PRAISE FOR *COURAGEOUS EDVENTURES*

"Jennie Magiera does a superb job of providing practical ideas and strategies on how to actually implement innovative practices in today's classroom. Her knowledge and experience as a change agent further strengthen the techniques presented and will help educators truly envision what's possible in classrooms today."

Eric Sheninger, Corwin Author and
Senior Fellow, International Center for Leadership in Education

"Jennie Magiera leads people on a great journey through this book with some great ideas to get started in the classroom right now, or the inspiration to find your own way leading to innovative ideas for learning and teaching. A great book for those wanting to bring innovation to life in their classrooms."

George Couros, Author of The Innovator's Mindset, *and*
Innovative Teaching, Learning, and Leadership Consultant

"This book is certainly courageous. Instead of offering a step-by-step guide for your next technology purchases, Jennie Magiera masterfully designed an ecology of learning that is rich not only in assorted learning technologies, but in learner experimentation, autonomy, collaboration, problem solving, reflection, and so much more. Her expansive approach to technology integration and the principles underlying it will be relevant for many years. Suffice to say, the ideas found on every page of this book will be just a as relevant a decade from now as they are today."

Curt Bonk, Professor at Indiana University, and
President of CourseShare, LLC

"Jennie Magiera guides teachers as they navigate obstacles to discover classroom innovation in her new book, *Courageous Edventures*. She starts off asking teachers to be courageous and bold because true progress and innovation only happens when they disrupt the status quo and take big risks. Jennie knows how daunting this is for teachers so she thoughtfully created strategies so any teacher can feel safe and comfortable embarking on this journey. The book is organized in four sections based on a sailing metaphor that helps teachers prepare for their Edventure, navigate problems, empower students to set their own course, and then reflect on the journey. I highly recommend teachers and administrators to read *Courageous Edventures* to guide them and encourage discussions around changing teaching practice."

Barbara Bray, Creative Learning Strategist and
Co-author of Make Learning Personal *and* How to Personalize Learning, *Oakland, CA*

"In *Courageous Edventures*, our innovative educaptain, Jennie Magiera, charts our course for the perfect blend of inspiration and practical and actionable ideas that can help to reinvigorate the classroom. A must read for new and veteran teachers alike that can remind us all why we teach."

Adam Bellow, Founder of EduTecher and EduClipper

"*Courageous Edventures* shares both inspiring tidbits and practical strategies for changing a school, a classroom, or a lesson. Magiera provides a valuable blend of personal stories and applicable examples for educators in any setting. I encourage educators to read the book and think about how they can be more courageous in their own practice."

Zachary Walker, Author of Teaching the Last Backpack Generation
National Institute of Education, Singapore

"*Courageous Edventures* is full of insightful and actionable ideas for transforming your classroom. Magiera paints a picture of innovative teaching and learning that is accessible for educators at all stages of their career. I love Magiera's student-centered approach to using technology to reach authentic audiences and the colorful stories from the classroom. This is a must-read for teachers searching for a road map for deeper learning!"

Monica Burns, Author and Speaker,
Apple Distinguished Educator, Founder of ClassTechTips.com

"Principals, superintendents, and other leaders in education, share this book with your teachers now. Magiera's thoughtful and delightful insight into the best of what's happening in our schools will inspire new teachers and reinvigorate veterans to provide the classroom experiences our students need to thrive in and shape their world."

Kevin Brookhouser, Author of The 20time Project:
How educators can launch Google's formula for future-ready innovation

"Magiera takes us on a Courageous Edventure by outlining a blueprint for charting a new course while navigating rough waters in order to sail into the Great Beyond. Her words of wisdom, stemming from her career as a practitioner, are encouraging yet simultaneously challenging—challenging educators to create new, authentic learning experiences for all kids. Whether your setting is urban, suburban, or rural, Magiera will push your thinking, challenge the status quo, and support your work in developing Future Ready classrooms and schools. *Courageous Edventures* is a great read and a needed tool for your toolbox!"

Thomas C. Murray, Director of Innovation
Future Ready Schools

"With *Courageous Edventures*, Jennie Magiera has created a book that is both powerful and accessible to teachers who want to transform their classrooms into more modern, active, empowering spaces. Magiera's powerful voice and passion for the work shine through on every page, making this a fun read as well as a deeply helpful read as well."

Chris Lehmann, Founding Principal of Science Leadership Academy and
Author of Building School 2.0

"This book is written for any educator looking to sail into an innovative classroom. Ms. Magiera uses humor and stories to identify with educators and help guide the reader through the transition of a traditional classroom to an innovative classroom. This book takes you on a journey and is packed with ideas, examples, and resources that would be invaluable to any educator."

Kelly Fitzgerald, Online Learning Integration Specialist
Leander ISD

"A practical and resource-filled guide to using technology to true advantage in the classroom."

Betsy Ruffin, Retired Educator, Technology Consultant
B Ruffin Enterprises, Cleburne, TX

"*Courageous Edventures* is as fun as it is wildly useful for teachers wanting to move from hope for more effective teaching and more satisfying professional experiences to realizing both. Magiera helpfully explores the general (building professional networks, reflecting collaboratively, etc.) and the specific (her brilliant "Gripe Jam," fascinating ways to use OK Go videos, and much more) in ways that will hold the attention of both veterans and newbies. This is a perfect book for those in teacher education programs and professional study teams at all kinds of schools."

Rushton Hurley, Educator and Executive Director
Next Vista for Learning

COURAGEOUS EDVENTURES

To Mom and Dad, *my first teachers:*

*Thank you for always challenging me to
be better, try harder, and love life.*

I miss you so much.

COURAGEOUS EDVENTURES

Navigating Obstacles to Discover Classroom Innovation

Jennie Magiera

CORWIN
A SAGE Publishing Company

FOR INFORMATION:

Corwin

A SAGE Company

2455 Teller Road

Thousand Oaks, California 91320

(800) 233-9936

www.corwin.com

SAGE Publications Ltd.

1 Oliver's Yard

55 City Road

London EC1Y 1SP

United Kingdom

SAGE Publications India Pvt. Ltd.

B 1/I 1 Mohan Cooperative Industrial Area

Mathura Road, New Delhi 110 044

India

SAGE Publications Asia-Pacific Pte. Ltd.

3 Church Street

#10-04 Samsung Hub

Singapore 049483

Acquisitions Editor: Ariel Bartlett

Senior Associate Editor: Desirée Bartlett

Senior Editorial Assistant: Andrew Olson

Production Editor: Amy Schroller

Copy Editor: Erin Livingston

Typesetter: C&M Digitals (P) Ltd.

Proofreader: Dennis W. Webb

Indexer: Karen Wiley

Cover Designer: Scott Van Atta

Marketing Manager: Anna Mesick

Library of Congress Cataloging-in-Publication Data

Names: Magiera, Jennie, author.

Title: Courageous edventures : navigating obstacles to discover classroom innovation / Jennie Magiera.

Description: Thousand Oaks, California : Corwin, 2016. | Includes index.

Identifiers: LCCN 2016025936 | ISBN 9781506318349 (pbk. : alk. paper)

Subjects: LCSH: Classroom management. | Educational technology. | Effective teaching.

Classification: LCC LB3013 .M275 2016 | DDC 371.102/4—dc23

LC record available at https://lccn.loc.gov/2016025936

This book is printed on acid-free paper.

Certified Chain of Custody

SUSTAINABLE FORESTRY INITIATIVE

Promoting Sustainable Forestry

www.sfiprogram.org

SFI-01268

SFI label applies to text stock

18 19 20 10 9 8 7 6 5 4 3

CONTENTS

Acknowledgments   xiii

About the Author   xv

Preface   xvii

PART I. CHARTING YOUR COURSE   **1**

1. Come on in, the Future's Fine   2
   Me and the Three Little Pigs   2
   From Houses to Ships   3
   What Is Innovation?   4
   Two Compass Options: The SAMR and TIM Frameworks   8
   Deciding When to Use SAMR and When to Use TIM   9
   Setting a Course for Innovation   12

2. Problem-Based Learning: It's Not Just for Kids   13
   Teacher Innovation Exploration Plan: An Individualized
        Education Program for Teachers   14
   Identifying the Problem of Practice   14
   Defining the Problem of Practice   21
   Stepping Up to a Solution   21
   Critical Friends   25

3. Getting Your Students Ready   27
   Learning to SAIL: Student Innovation Teams   27
      Don't Touch   29
      Go Slow   29
      Be Kind   29
   Staying Safe on the Open Sea: Digital Citizenship   32
      What Is Digital Citizenship?   32
      Respect for Ourselves   32
      Respect for Others   37

4. Getting Your Materials Ready — 39

Let the Students Lead the Way — 39

Build a Management System — 40

Rewrite Your Supply List — 42

Tech Is Not a Treat — 44

Less Is More — 46

5. Falling in Love With Failure — 47

Calling Forth Your Courage — 47

Failing Forward — 48

Student Failure — 49

Teacher Failure — 50

System Failure — 52

PART II. NAVIGATING YOUR PROBLEMS — **55**

6. Digging Into Differentiation — 56

Problem: So Many Ability Groups, So Little Time — 56

Suggestion: Clone the Teacher — 57

Problem: Keeping Students Engaged During Small-Group Time — 60

Suggestion 1: Choose Your Own Adventure Time — 60

Suggestion 2: Self-Differentiating Challenges — 61

Suggestion 3: Critical Friends — 64

Problem: Finding Developmentally
Appropriate Differentiated Content — 64

Suggestion 1: Create Your Own Content — 64

Suggestion 2: Digital Resources — 65

Problem: How Do I Disseminate Materials to
Students and Collect Their Work? (aka Digital Workflow) — 65

Suggestion 1: Learning Management System — 65

Suggestion 2: Google Classroom — 66

Suggestion 3: Class Websites, QR Codes, and Google Forms — 66

7. Rethinking Assessment — 67

Problem: I Hate Grading! — 67

Suggestion 1: Digital Student Response Software — 67

Suggestion 2: Learning Management Systems Assessments — 68

Suggestion 3: Online Forms — 69

Problem: I Need to Differentiate Assessments Based on Individualized
Education Program Accommodations and/or Modifications — 69

Suggestion: Screencast Assessments 69

Problem: My Students Have a Hard Time Self-Assessing 70

Suggestion 1: Metacognitive Screencasting 70

Suggestion 2: Digital Portfolios 72

The Draw of Google Drawings 75

Problem: Teaching Students How to Give Peer Feedback 78

Suggestion 1: Google Drive 78

Suggestion 2: Google Drive and Google Forms 80

Suggestion 3: Blogging and Quadblogging 80

Accountability Without Assessment:
Gamification and Achievement Badges 80

8. Creating a Positive Classroom Environment 86

Problem: Creating a Culture of Respect and Collaboration 86

Suggestion 1: Mood Check-Ins 87

Suggestion 2: Class Dojo for Encouraging Positive Action 88

Suggestion 3: Using Music to Set the Mood 89

Problem: Supporting Struggling Students 91

Suggestion 1: Blogging 91

Suggestion 2: Positivity Timelines 91

Problem: Communicating With Families 92

Suggestion 1: Class Dojo for Communication 93

Suggestion 2: Google Forms 93

Suggestion 3: Digital Newsletters/Class Blog 95

9. Planning for Powerful Learning 96

Problem: Finding Curricular Resources 96

Suggestion 1: Pinterest and EduClipper 96

Suggestion 2: Twitter and Google+ 97

Suggestion 3: Blogs! 98

Problem: Scheduling Time for
Collaborative Team Planning 98

Suggestion 1: Google Calendar 98

Suggestion 2: Doodle.com 98

Suggestion 3: Google Hangouts 99

Problem: Vertical Alignment—What's
the Rest of the School Teaching? 99

Suggestion 1: Google Drive 99

Suggestion 2: Shared Calendars 100

PART III. SAILING INTO THE GREAT BEYOND   **103**

10. Power to the Pupil   104

    Cultivate Curiosity: How Do I Build Curiosity?   107

        Sorting Your Questions: Questdones and Questruns   107

    Outwit Obstacles: How Do I Teach Perseverance?   110

    Purposeful Playtime: How Do I Find the Time for Purposeful Play?   115

        Reimagined Centers   116

        20% Time   116

        Open Scheduling   116

        Bringing the Purpose to the Playtime: Entering Creation Station   117

        Reflect, Reflect, Reflect   119

11. Discovering the Power of Voice   121

    Amplifying Our Students   121

    Step 1: Finding Their Inner Voice—Blogs Versus Diaries   123

    Step 2: Sharing Their Voice With Others—Building Classroom Discussions and Backchanneling   126

    Step 3: Teacher-Moderated Sharing—Dipping a Toe Into Social Media   129

    Step 4: Opening the Garden Walls—Diving Into Social Media   131

12. With Great Power Comes Great Responsibility   133

    Revisiting Problem-Based Learning   133

    Digging in to Problem-Based Learning   134

        Step 1: Finding the Problem-Based Essential Question   135

        Step 2: Developing the Challenge   136

        Step 3: Rising to the Challenge   137

        Step 4: Showcasing the Learning   138

    The Role of the Teacher   138

    Problem-Based Learning Spotlight—KidTREK: A Safe Journey App for Students   139

    The Student Becomes the Master   140

PART IV. REFLECTING ON YOUR EDVENTURE   **143**

13. Evaluating Your Practice   144

    Looping in Your Critical Friend   144

    Revisiting the SAMR and TIM Frameworks   144

    Leveling Up With the SAMR Model   145

    Approaching the Three Dimensions of the TIM   146

Sharing Your Adventure 146
Taking It a Step Further: Presenting Your Story 149

14. Staying Inspired and Finding Support 151
  Creating a Professional Learning Network That Works 151
    Professional Learning Communities
      and Professional Learning Networks 151
    Cultivating Constructive Conflict 152
    A Shared Space 152
  Teacher-Led Learning Events 153
    EdCamps 154
    PLAYDATEs 154
  Formal Learning Events 157
    Step 1: Go With a Goal in Mind 158
    Step 2: Keep a Three-Dance Card 158
    Step 3: Recruit Allies and Use Collaborative Tools 158
    Step 4: Schedule Time With Yourself to Debrief Individually 159
    Step 5: Pay It Forward 159

15. Planning Your Next Edventure 162
  Be Your Own Hero 163
  Don't Get Comfortable 163
  Channel Your Inner Student 163
  Share Your Crazy Pills 164

Appendix A: Challenge Card Template 165

Appendix B: Teacher Innovation Exploration Plan (TIEP) 166

Index 169

To continue your edventures online,
please visit the companion website.
http://resources.corwin.com/courageousedventures

ACKNOWLEDGMENTS

To my all of my students, past, present, and future—thank you for allowing me to help you grow and learn. You're the reason I do what I do every day.

To my professional learning community—thank you for sharing your inspiration, passion, and love of education with me. We're better together, and I'm better because of you. Without this amazing network of educator friends, I wouldn't have the courage and confidence to edventure.

To the many who shared feedback and encouragement on this book as it was being developed, written, rewritten, and rewritten again—thank you for being so generous with your time and support.

To all of my friends and family—thank you for always being there with encouraging words, big hugs, and infinite love.

To my sister, Katherine: Thank you for being my little sister and big hero. You're the author I hope to be; I'm your biggest fan. Mom and Dad would have been so proud of you, as I am. *"And I love you very much."*

And of course, to my husband, Jim: You're the love of my life, my best friend and other half. You make me smile every day and make me a better version of myself. I'm happiest when I'm with you. *"I love you, have a nice day."*

Publisher's Acknowledgments

Corwin gratefully acknowledges the contributions of the following reviewers:

Marisa Burvikovs
Fifth/Sixth Grade Talent Development Teacher
LaGrange School District 102
Brookfield, IL

Sandra Burvikovs
K–5 Gifted Education Teacher
Lake Zurich Community School District 95
Lake Zurich, IL

Julie Duford
Fifth Grade Teacher, Presidential Awardee in Mathematics
Polson Middle School
Polson, MT

Kelly Fitzgerald
Online Learning Integration Specialist
Leander ISD
Leander, TX

Carol S. Holzberg
Director of Technology
Greenfield Public Schools
Greenfield, MA

Betsy Ruffin
Retired Educator, Technology Consultant
B Ruffin Enterprises
Cleburne, TX

Bill Singer
EdTech Integration Specialist
Santa Rosa, CA

Pam Turley
Technology Curriculum Specialist
Nebo School District
Spanish Fork, UT

About the Author

 Jennie Magiera always knew she wanted to be a teacher when she grew up. Throughout all of her roles, starting as a Chicago Public Schools teacher to currently serving as the Chief Technology Officer for Des Plaines School District 62, she has always made teaching and supporting students her priority. A White House Champion for Change, Apple Distinguished Educator, Google for Education Certified Innovator, and TEDx Speaker, Jennie works to improve teaching and learning through innovative new practices. She is also passionate about transforming professional learning, which she's personally championed through her work as an international speaker, member of the Technical Working Group for the U.S. Department of Education's 2016 National Educational Technology Plan and cofounding PLAYDATE as well as other new conference concepts. Jennie has earned degrees from Phillips Exeter Academy, Columbia University, and University of Illinois–Chicago. Aside from her students, Jennie's great loves in life are sci-fi, mashed potatoes, Tabasco sauce, her dog, and her husband. You can find Jennie on Twitter at @MsMagiera or through her blog, *Teaching Like It's 2999.*

PREFACE

Don't be satisfied with stories, how things have gone with others.
Unfold your own myth.

—Rumi

Will you join me on an adventure? We must be courageous. We must be bold. As educators, we hope for limitless possibilities for our students. However, too often we are told what we can't do, given restrictions, and trapped into boxed curricula. Everyone's an expert on education because everyone went to school. The rhetoric is about avoiding failure and maintaining the steady plod toward increasing test scores. Yet true progress and innovation is achieved when brave individuals disrupt the status quo and take big risks.

To go on our adventure, we need to be brave enough to sail in new directions. This means embracing the possibility of failure, preparing for potential storms and inevitable rocky shores. It means taking a set of fresh eyes to chart a course around the many challenges, the naysayers, and the wall builders. This is possible. We can break free from the blockade of negativity to dream bigger for our kids. The good news is that others have already embarked on this journey and have left us clues on how to follow. In fact, the story of daring exploration becoming accessible to all is a tale that has been repeated throughout history.

Over 3,000 years ago, Polynesian ancestors set out in canoes to sail across the ocean and discover new worlds using nothing but the stars, water, and wind to guide them (see Figure 0.1). As the voyagers sailed off, the majority of their brethren remained on land, watching and waiting to see how they fared. Perhaps those left behind wanted to go along but couldn't for lack of vessels. Perhaps they wanted to follow but feared the hazards. Perhaps they thought these adventurers were completely bananas and wanted no business in that adventuring nonsense. However, when the early explorers returned, it became clear that there were increased opportunities just over the horizon. So the explorers shared their discoveries, described the path, and encouraged others to follow.

FIGURE 0.1 Polynesian Sailors

SOURCE: Public Domain. John Webber—Alexander Turnbull Library

We are experiencing a similar pattern today in education. The early innovators have already set out on a course to discover new possibilities for their students across the digital sea. Of those who didn't partake in this endeavor, some wanted to join but couldn't for lack of devices or connectivity. Some were intrigued but hesitated due to the many challenges. Still others simply weren't sold on the idea. Now that the early innovators have gone forth, have succeeded, and are sharing the stories of increased student opportunity, we are drawn to follow. But what of the hazards we may encounter: the many obstacles facing students, teachers, and schools that seem to prevent passage toward innovative learning? Fear of these hazards stops many from even attempting the first step. This book will help you both face and overcome those obstacles so you may embark on your own edventure.

I remember my first edventure. On July 29, 2010, I was getting ready for bed and decided to check my e-mail. As I read through my messages, I burst into tears—big, melodramatic sobs. My husband peered over my shoulder to see what I was reading and exclaimed, "Oh, congratulations, honey! You got the iPad grant! Look at you, crying because you're so happy." As he pulled me in for a congratulatory hug, I sullenly corrected him. "No, Jim. I'm not crying because I'm happy. I'm crying because now I actually have to do all the garbage I made up in the grant. I have no idea what I'm doing."

You see, I wasn't what you would call an "early adopter" at this point in my life or career. I had never seen an iPad in real life. In fact, I may have openly teased my friends who purchased one, congratulating them on buying a soon-to-be outdated "giant iPhone that can't even make calls." I wrote this grant because it was something new, something different for my students. I had a vague notion of the possibilities that it could unleash but no clear idea of how to set forth in that direction. The grant I had written was riddled with impossibilities—some actually impossible (i.e., the many Flash-based websites I claimed I would use that could not run on an iPad) and some seemingly impossible (i.e., I would automatically differentiate for each student individually at all times of the day through the use of iPads.) The sweet irony was that since the concept of iPads in education was so new—this was only a few months after the iPad was publicly released—the folks who reviewed my grant also had little idea of how this would look.

And so that August, they wheeled a cart of 32 iPads into my classroom. At first, my experience was both terrifying and confusing. I spent endless hours after school trying to figure out "how to iPad." After several months of trial and error, I realized that I was focusing on the wrong thing. I began to understand that my goal shouldn't simply be to do something new for the sake of it being new or to get better at using these new tools. Rather, my focus should be to solve existing problems with new methodologies—and in the process, to reimagine how teaching and learning could look and feel like. The iPads weren't the destination. They were a *vehicle* for reaching existing goals.

Although this realization was huge, I was still daunted by the challenge of figuring out where to begin, what first steps to make, and what risks to take. I wrote this book to be the compass and guide I wish I had at that time. It is also the guide I wish I had in my current role as a support to thousands of teachers making the same journey that I once took. It encompasses the learning experiences I had through failure and iteration, crowdsourcing and collaboration, research and exploration.

This book is for educators endeavoring to make a tangible and positive impact on teaching and learning through technology use. Whether you have a device in the hands of every student or nothing but a laptop and projector or you're simply looking toward the future, this is your partner in inspiration and "I can do this" ideas. As a teacher, I rarely found time to sit down and read long professional texts. Keeping this in mind, I've filled this book with images, diagrams, lesson ideas, and resources that you can download for use immediately. Moreover, the format of the book is set up so you can use it as a quick reference to solve certain problems or follow it as a step-by-step guide to transform your practice.

HOW TO USE THIS BOOK

These chapters are organized into four sections—Part I: "Charting Your Course," Part II: "Navigating Your Problems", Part III: "Sailing Into the

Great Beyond" and Part IV: "Reflecting on Your Edventure." You can read through from beginning to end to chronologically steer each step of your odyssey. However, you can also simply pick up the book, find what you need, and dig in immediately.

Part I: "Charting Your Course" sets the foundation and focus for your work. It is about preparing for the edventure: setting up your room, students, devices, and mindset. The concept of problem-based innovation (PBI) is explained and you will learn how to create your own Teacher Innovation Exploration Plan (TIEP). This will be the focus document to help you plan and chart your progress.

Part II: "Navigating Your Problems" prepares you for the edventure by first identifying and navigating around the problems that currently exist to formulate your TIEP. They are the nagging "yes, but . . ." you hear in the back of your mind when thinking of attempting something risky. This section is set up in a problem–solution structure with a litany of educational problems listed by category. For each problem, there are various suggestions offered. If you're looking to dive into a digital renovation of your room, you can set focus goals through Part I by creating your TIEP and then use this section to look for solution ideas.

Part III: "Sailing Into the Great Beyond" takes advantage of your "cleared waters" from Part II to push onward into the next frontier of classroom innovation. In this realm, you learn to hand over the wheel to your students and empower them to set their own course for learning. This is the meatiest part of the book, as it explores the power of student agency as well as the forethought and process needed to successfully support it.

Part IV: "Reflecting on Your Edventure" is about how you can reflect upon and share your experience (and even plan the next). Once you've finished reading this book, where can you find additional help? How can you continue to audit and improve your practice? Here, I share some tips and ideas that I use on a regular basis to continue learning and growing in order to become a better version of myself.

So come on board, and hold on tight, because we're heading off for an edventure to change your classroom . . . and perhaps the world while we're at it.

Disclaimer About the Tools Mentioned in This Book

Pepsi or Coke? Mac or PC? Burger King or McDonalds? With brand rivalries like these, people tend to pick their team and stick with it. I've witnessed patrons sending back drinks when they order a Coke and instead receive a Pepsi. I've seen friends venomously arguing about which phone platform reigns supreme. It seems that they are married to their brand choice—and for many, this comes with a fierce loyalty.

The same seems to go with educational technology rivalries. iPads or Chromebooks? Edmodo or Schoology? AppleTV or Chromecast? In these cases, I was once a staunch advocate for or adversary against one program, site, or device. I thought these loyalties were forever. And yet, as I spend longer in the constantly evolving landscape that is educational technology, I am discovering a new truth: There are no long-term relationships in educational technology. I may be a believer in Brand A or Device B one month, but the next month—or even sometimes the next week—something new will come about that will tip the ship and I find myself switching teams.

Therefore, the tools mentioned in this book are temporally bound. They are relevant and recommended as of the date I wrote about them. However, things change. So the challenge I had was to write a book that will remain mostly static over time about a landscape that is ever changing. My response was twofold:

1. Write about pedagogy, not tools. For the most part, the ideas posed in this book are about philosophies, strategies, and learning—not the tools. When there are tools mentioned, they are given as an example of what's out there right now. As I mention frequently throughout the book, the learning opportunities are point, not the tools.

2. Provide a companion website with updated lists of tools, features, and ideas. The companion website can be found at http://resources.corwin.com/courageoused ventures. There are QR codes throughout this book to reach the corresponding webpage or resource.

In addition to taking this approach, I want to leave you with three tips on how to audit the educational technology tools you encounter, both those you will find in these pages and those you are already using.

Tip #1: Embrace the Competition

Competition in some forms can definitely be ugly. Yet, in the case of competing companies, they can boost progress. When the iPhone first came out, it was the only one of its kind. It was, by default, best in its class. Then, as the Android and Windows smartphones started to improve, they pushed iOS developers to rethink their approach and up the ante. The big teams had to think outside of the box that their competitors created . . . and so the box grew bigger. As spoiled consumers used to the bigger and the better, this works out quite nicely. As educators used to glacial progress when it comes to learning tools, this is incredibly refreshing and exciting. Finally, teachers are the recipients of a speedy improvement loop.

(Continued)

Tip #2: Consistently Audit What You Think You Know

As a result of this competition, these products are constantly updating. A product that was once subpar or missing a key feature can become the best fit for your needs overnight. For example, I used to harbor strong negative feelings toward a certain learning management system while favoring another. Then a large site update occurred, and I was forced to reevaluate my stance. I must admit that it's hard to keep up; as everything is constantly changing, nothing is ever set in stone. This can be frustrating when we're used to learning something and then relying on that knowledge as we move through our work. Despite this, taking time to regularly revisit tools you think you know, or ones you've previously dismissed, can prove incredibly fruitful.

Tip #3: Loyalty to Students Over All Else

At the end of the day, it isn't about brand loyalty. It's about what is best for our students. I used to feel bad about switching from one product to another. I thought of myself as a "fill-in-the-blank brand" person. But when it comes to choosing devices or programs for educational use, that all goes out the window. We shouldn't be loyal to brands; we need to be loyal to our students. When selecting an instructional tool, we need to be asking, "What can solve our problems of practice? What can push our pedagogy? What is going to provide the best user experience and opportunity for my students to succeed?" And if those answers change from one week to another, that's okay, as long as it's our students who are benefiting.

part I

CHARTING YOUR COURSE

A ship in harbor is safe, but that is not what ships are built for.

—John A. Shedd

chapter 1

COME ON IN, THE FUTURE'S FINE

Oh, hello! Thank you for joining me on this voyage! I'm so glad to have you along as a fellow edventurer. You may be feeling a bit nervous. Have heart and ignore any nagging voices telling you this journey is foolhardy, whether they are real or in your head. Remember, we must be courageous. Others have gone before us and they have survived the crossing. Every day we're in school, it's an endeavor—today, we've simply decided to go in a different direction. You can do this.

The first step in our edventure is charting a course. This is tricky because while others have sailed ahead, we can't follow the exact same path. Your classroom is unique to you and your students. As such, so are your needs and route toward innovation. Thus, before we set sail, we need make sure we are clear on our ultimate destination. We need to understand: What is innovation, really? To aid us in finding the answer, I want to tell you a story.

ME AND THE THREE LITTLE PIGS

We've all heard the story of the three little pigs. They each had their own way of evading the big bad wolf—one built a house out of sticks, another of straw, and one out of bricks. Spoiler alert if you're the lone soul who hasn't heard this fairy tale: The brick house wins.

But what we don't consider when telling this story is that the brick-building piggy was a bit of an early innovator. He decided to go against the grain and try out a new technology: bricks. His pig brethren scoffed at him: They said it would be more difficult to use this material; they were just fine the way they were.

However, let's try rewriting this story so that all the pigs have a fair chance at survival. Let's say that the other two piggies won a grant for some state-of-the-art bricks. They see that bricks are leading to extended pig-longevity and so decide to jump on the bandwagon and "innovate." They wheel their cart of bricks up to their stick and straw houses and think, "But I love my straw windows. And my stick foyer is what I'm comfortable with. I've lived this way for years and it's worked for me. But they say bricks are better. I guess I have to use them."

So, wanting to use the bricks but not wanting to change their structure, the two little pigs just duct tape the bricks to their stick and straw structures. You don't need to be a structural engineer to know what happens when you duct tape bricks to sticks and straw. Yup, the houses collapse. The wolf eats the pigs. The End.

I don't tell you this fractured fairy tale to make you sad. It's a metaphor for what I did when I first got my shiny new "innovative tools." The iPads arrived a few days before my students, and I quickly made plans to integrate them into the structure of my classroom. Throughout that fall, a casual observer would have witnessed my students glued to a sea of glistening tablets. It all looked great. But the effects were superficial.

The iPads were not helping my students make substantial progress toward self-efficacy, academic achievement, or social-emotional growth. After weeks of frustration and little tangible progress, I took a step back and asked myself, "What have we been doing so far with this technology?" Students used math apps instead of math card games. They logged onto websites that showed them instructional cartoons and quizzed their knowledge. They'd annotated a few PDFs of short nonfiction texts. They'd done some research on the Internet. In short, things were going . . . OK. Things were different in my classroom, certainly. But just as certain was the fact that things were no *better* than before the technology rolled in.

The problem, I began to realize, was my own understanding of the role of technology in our classroom. I had seen it as a supplement to my preexisting curriculum, trying to fit it into the structure of what I'd always done. Like those piggies, I was trying to duct tape these new tools onto my straw house.

As terrifying as it may sound, I had to find the courage to take a proverbial sledge-hammer to my existing classroom framework. This realization was a turning point for me. I would have to be willing to depart from what I had always done or always taught. I needed to create a blueprint for a fresh classroom design with the power of my new tools in mind. By setting aside my preconceived notions of how my classroom "should" look, sound, and feel, I was able to transform my practice from the ground up. Finally, I was ready to innovate.

FROM HOUSES TO SHIPS

Now take this metaphor of technology being the powerful new building blocks for our classroom and imagine that instead of building houses, we're building something more mobile, like ships. Technology becomes the building blocks for better, faster vehicles that can help our students sail to realms of increased opportunity. Until now, we've been floating on rafts. We've been at the whim of the fickle tides of educational politics and testing. At best, we've been able to tether to stagnant buoys in the form of big-box curriculum companies. We haven't been given the freedom to truly *sail*.

Once we have digital devices to become our powerful ships, we must find a destination to which to sail. No, technology isn't the destination—mastering it is not the goal. Remember, technology is your *vehicle*. The *destination* is that elusive concept: Innovation.

WHAT IS INNOVATION?

Innovation has become an overused word across many industries. Education is no exception. A basic Internet book search for *education innovation* yields over 17,000 titles. In fact, I was hesitant to include the word in my own title for fear of sounding cliché. Yet I believe in the concept of innovation and posit that we have only begun to touch the surface on understanding its application in schools. Many people in education tend to use the word *innovation* to refer to the digital transformation or the increased use of technology in school settings. However, this focuses on a minute aspect of educational innovation. So let's start with the basics and ask, "What is innovation?" To respond to this, I have three points:

(1) **Innovation is not only different but also better.** According to Merriam-Webster, innovation is "the act or process of introducing new ideas, devices, or methods." I don't think that many would disagree with this meaning. Yet we should be cautious, as *new* is easily misconstrued as *better* and that's not always the case. *New* does not always necessarily infer *and improved*. Recall product flops such as LaserDisc, New Coke, and BetaMax. While these all sounded exciting and different at their onset, they didn't effectively improve upon the original idea.

In the realm of education, innovation is about solving old problems with new and *better* ideas. It's one of the reasons the word is popping up more often these days—we have new tools to utilize in our classrooms and therefore new opportunities to solve our problems. We must be careful that the focus doesn't shift from bettering our situations to just using tools. Many educators share this view of educational innovation. In fact, George Couros in his book, *The Innovator's Mindset*, writes at length about this specific definition. "Innovation can come from either 'invention' (something totally new) or 'iteration' (a change of something that already exists), but if it does not meet the idea of new and better,' it is not innovative."[1] So as we embark on our journey to innovate in our educational space, we want to consistently be auditing our practice by asking ourselves, "Is the new also improved?"

(2) **Innovation is personal.** To illustrate this point, let's posit a scenario: Suppose two women alone on two separate yet identical ships were lost at sea. Dying of thirst, they both searched for ways to create fresh water using the exact same materials. They both came up with the same new and incredible

---

[1]Couros, G. (2015). *The innovator's mindset*. Dave Burgess Consulting.

idea. However, the woman on Ship A came up with it before the woman on Ship B. Does that make the woman on Ship B's idea any less innovative? Is something less innovative if someone else has done it before?

Let's take it a step further to say that Ms. Ship B didn't actually come up with the idea on her own but somehow heard about Ms. Ship A's breakthrough and then decided to try it out. True, Ms. Ship B won't get credit for the idea itself, but does that make her decision to utilize it and the positive change on her life any less impactful?

Just because something is old hat to one person doesn't mean that it isn't life changing to someone else. For example, finding a way to instantly share student work with families may seem mundane to teachers that have digital portfolio platforms and learning management tools, but it may make a huge difference for teachers with neither previous access to nor knowledge of these tools.

In the past, I used to judge the level or validity of innovative practices in and around our schools. As I worked with teachers, I would deem some of forays into digital practices to be low-level concepts while others were higher ranking. What I forgot to take into account was the personal situations and circumstances of each teacher and his or her students. I began to realize that rather than judging the innovation level of a colleague as an outsider, I needed to be a reflective partner to help the teacher make that assessment on his or her own.

When pursuing innovation within your classroom, you should be able to identify your own unique challenges and explore what different and better ideas are out there to combat them. Whether the world deems these ideas innovative shouldn't matter. If they are truly creating different and better opportunities for you and your students, it's innovation to you.

(3) **Innovation shouldn't be a luxury (but it is).** As I visit schools and districts across the U.S. and beyond, something has become evident to me: The ability to innovate is a luxury. Some schools can afford it and others cannot. By this, I don't just mean the financial burden of purchasing devices. I refer to the political and temporal burden of scripted curricula and test-driven school culture. Some schools—often private, high-achieving public, or charter schools—allow for a certain level of teacher autonomy, risk taking, and creativity when shaping their student learning.

Other schools—too often, those in rural or urban areas or those serving at-risk youth—face a myriad of pressures (test scores, district mandates, etc.) and thus restrict these choices by applying a high level of oversight on what, how, and when things must be taught. As a result, the gap continues to grow between schools actively exploring new methods to improve teaching and learning and schools passively using digital tools for the sake of the tools. The latter usually takes the form of low-level drill-and-kill programs that do little to inspire or engage our students (but rather drill and kill any curiosity out of them). The 2016 U.S. Department of Education's National Education Technology Plan calls this difference the Digital Use Divide[2] (see Figure 1.1).

However, there is a third group of schools: those that face the challenges of high-stakes testing as well as other pressures and still permit teachers the freedom to try new methodologies and give them the space to fail forward. These schools usually have a leader at the helm that understands and embraces the potential student benefits for allowing room for innovation. I was lucky to be a teacher in one of these schools.

In 2006, my principal, Amy Rome, encouraged the teachers at National Teachers Academy to take charge of not only our classrooms but to become leaders in the school itself. Despite the fact that at the time, our student population was over 95% low-income and we were struggling to raise test scores to meet district and state requirements, she believed that empowering teachers to empower their students was a key part of the equation—not drill-and-kill lesson sets. As a result, I had the rare opportunity to explore the world of inner-city innovation. I deviated from the scripted curriculum and took risks and my students began to thrive. Whereas workshops, trainings, and literature told me that my students

FIGURE 1.1 The Digital Use Divide

DIGITAL **USE** DIVIDE

While essential, closing the digital divide alone will not transform learning. We must also close the digital **use** divide by ensuring all students understand how to use technology as a tool to engage in creative, productive, life-long learning rather than simply consuming passive content.

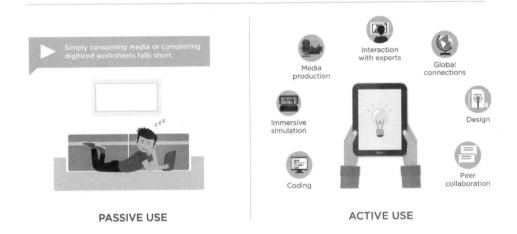

PASSIVE USE   ACTIVE USE

[2]Office of Educational Technology. (n.d.). *National education technology plan.* Retrieved from http://tech.ed.gov/netp

needed a highly regulated day, a "rigorous program" (read: scripted curricula), and increased structure, I found exactly the opposite. The more freedom I gave my class, the more effort and progress they made. The more opportunities for choice I gave them, the more often they made positive choices.

Innovation shouldn't be a luxury given only to those schools that can politically afford to give their teachers the time and space to take risks. And yet it is. So what can we do?

To classroom teachers in a setting without the freedom to experiment who are reading this: Don't despair. As you move through these pages, you'll hopefully find kernels of hope in some of the simple ideas that you do have the power to implement. It may take longer to see the transformation, but these mini tweaks will build into something bigger over time. An inch forward is still moving in the right direction, so don't stop yourself because the impact seems too small. Remember the point above—innovation is personal. To the outside world, the changes may seem small, but for you and your students, it could make all the difference.

To school leaders in these settings, consider how you can encourage teachers to try new things and empower them with the belief that taking risks and attempting innovation is worthy of their time and effort. Hopefully this book can give you a few ideas to explore and disseminate. Know that you don't have to implement everything overnight or in all aspects of your school setting. As you read this book, look for ideas to try, methods to share, and areas of the school day in which you might give more space for teacher collaboration and risk taking.

To those classroom teachers lucky enough to be in a setting where you have the freedom and will to dive into innovation, *share your story* (see Part III for ideas on how to do this). The more voices and examples of positive change that can be had through educators taking risks and changing the educational narrative, the better!

Regardless of your circumstances, know that just because there is the freedom or the will to innovate doesn't mean it's always happening. Remember, when I began my quest to innovate I had both—and yet, at first, I failed to reach innovation in any sense of the word. Hopefully reading this book will help you visualize your destination a bit better so you won't have to turn around and start over as I did.

To avoid losing sight of your target, frequently check your progress and consider this: Is where you are today a different and better place than yesterday? Are you moving? If so, are you moving in the right direction? Remember, just as ships can help you sail toward a wondrous land of innovation, they can also get blown off course and wind up in a place worse off than where you started. So make sure you have a compass to check your course and heading. Below are two options to serve as that compass.

TWO COMPASS OPTIONS:
THE SAMR AND TIM FRAMEWORKS

FIGURE 1.2 The SAMR Model[3]

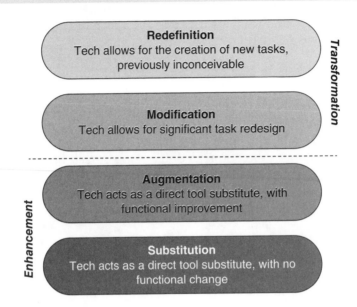

The SAMR Model, shown in Figure 1.2, is a simple framework to measure the impact of digital tools, created by Dr. Ruben Puentedura in the 1980s. The name is an acronym that represents the four stages of this scale: substitution, augmentation, modification, and redefinition. What's interesting about this model is that it doesn't focus on the improvement of the **tool** but rather the **goal** that the tool is attempting to achieve.

- At the **substitution** level, you're simply swapping out the analog tool for a parallel digital one. There is no real improvement to the task or its ability to meet the goal. For example, if a student is writing a letter with pencil and paper, a substitution-level activity would be typing it on a word processor, then printing it out and mailing it.
- At the **augmentation** level, the digital tool is improving on the analog tool without changing the task itself. For example, think of sending the letter via e-mail—you're still typing up a letter, it's just getting there faster.
- At the **modification** level, you begin to change the task itself. Instead of e-mailing a letter, you are video chatting in real time, improving the speed and efficacy at which you can communicate and also introducing a new visual dynamic.

---

[3]Puentedura. http://hippasus.com/blog/

- At the ultimate level of this model—**redefinition**—the task itself is completely transformed, providing a way to meet the goal that would be otherwise impossible without the technology. In this case, you may be video chatting not only with one person but with many and integrating other mediums such as collaborative drawing/writing/planning spaces, interactive media, or accessibility supports like live translation software or subtitles for the hearing impaired.

As you move through the SAMR model, it's important to note that the first two stages, *substitution* and *augmentation*, are in the enhancement level. They are simply adding onto the existing strategy or task. Once you reach the third and fourth stages, *modification* and *redefinition*, you are at the transformation level. At this point, you begin to change the task or strategy itself so as to improve on its efficacy to meet the goal.

If you are looking for a more complex model, consider the Technology Integration Matrix (TIM)[4] developed by the Florida Center for Instructional Technology at the University of South Florida. As seen in Figure 1.3,[5] this matrix is a continuum, just as the SAMR model, that helps educators reflect on their use of digital tools to improve learning. However, this is a three-dimensional matrix, with the three variables being learning environment, curricular technology integration level, and the object of transformation—student activity, teacher activity, or environment (in each cell). The vertical axis lists the five characteristics of a meaningful learning environment; the horizontal axis lists the five levels of technology integration into the curriculum. Each row and column header in the matrix opens into its own table, drilling down into descriptors for how these levels change the students, teachers, and the environment. While the tool has four versions that can be printed out as PDFs, it's much more robust as a digital tool. You can click on each cell within the matrix to find more detailed descriptors as well as video examples of in various content areas modeling the different levels and characteristics. This is a tool that takes a bit more getting used to, but it provides a wealth of details and guidance to support self-reflection.

DECIDING WHEN TO USE
SAMR AND WHEN TO USE TIM

Both SAMR and TIM are incredibly helpful tools for their own unique reasons. I have used and continue to use both in my practice. SAMR has been

---

[4]Florida Center for Instructional Technology. (2016). *The technology integration matrix*. Retrieved from http://fcit.usf.edu/matrix/

[5]The Technology Integration Matrix was developed by the Florida Center for Instructional Technology at the University of South Florida College of Education and funded with grants from the Florida Department of Education. For more information, visit http://mytechmatrix.org.

FIGURE 1.3 Technology Integration Matrix

Levels of Technology Integration Into the Curriculum

Characteristics of the Learning Environment

	Entry	Adoption	Adaption	Infusion	Transformation
Active	Information passively received	Conventional, procedural use of tools	Conventional independent use of tools; some student choice and exploration	Choice of tools and regular, self-directed use	Extensive and unconventional use of tools
Collaborative	Individual student use of tools	Collaborative use of tools in conventional ways	Collaborative use of tools; some student choice and exploration	Choice of tools and regular use for collaboration	Collaboration with peers and outside resources in ways not possible without technology
Constructive	Information delivered to students	Guided, conventional use for building knowledge	Independent use for building knowledge; some student choice and exploration	Choice and regular use for building knowledge	Extensive and unconventional use of technology tools to build knowledge
Authentic	Use unrelated to the world outside of the instructional setting	Guided use in activities with some meaningful context	Independent use in activities connected to students' lives; some student choice and exploration	Choice of tools and regular use in meaningful activities	Innovative use for higher order learning activities in a local or global context
Goal-Directed	Directions given, step-by-step task monitoring	Conventional and procedural use of tools to plan or monitor	Purposeful use of tools to plan and monitor; some student choice and exploration	Flexible and seamless use of tools to plan and monitor	Extensive and higher order use of tools to plan and monitor

SOURCE: Used with permission from the Florida Center for Instructional Technology, fcit.usf.edu

most helpful in getting started. When I want a straightforward framework to explain to a colleague how to reflect upon her practice and keep on course toward that different and better innovation, I introduce the SAMR model. It's not as intimidating and can be printed out—a great scaffold for someone who is already stymied by digital tools. Together, we take a look at the circumstances in her classroom—her students, families, curriculum, school/

district expectations, standards, and so on. Then we look at the challenges we're trying to solve and the new methods we're attempting. The SAMR model allows us to put a lens on these new methods to answer the following questions: Is this solution better than what I was doing before? If not, is it worth the time and tech (substitution)? If so, how? Is it doing the following?

- Improving on the original task but keeping the task the same (augmentation)
- Changing the task itself for the better (modification)
- Completely reimaging the task in a positive way that was previously inconceivable without the tool (redefinition)

If you're concerned that your focus may stray too easily away from the teaching and too much toward the tool, you may want to use TIM instead. Since this model is rooted in instructional language, its very indicators and descriptors force you to keep learning at the center. In fact, one of the transformation-level descriptors specifically advocate for this: "The technology tools become an invisible part of the learning" (Transformation Level Integration/Active Learning Environment/Student Activity).

This is also the model I would use if I were working with a teacher who has already dipped his toes into the water but wants to push himself further. It drills down deeper by descriptor and allows you to look at more finite aspects of your instruction. For example, how much choice are you giving students in selecting the tool they use to meet an instructional goal? How does technology facilitate more higher-order thinking in your classroom? And if you aren't sure what this looks like, the videos embedded within the matrix (though a bit dated at this point) provide a basic idea of these concepts in action.

Regardless of which framework you use, here are two things to keep in mind:

1. **Focus on the practice, not the tools.** As mentioned several times already (and will continue to be mentioned), it's all too easy to lose sight of the forest through the trees. Even if you begin with a focus on pedagogy and student learning, this can quickly turn into a quest for finding the perfect app or improving a particular digital skill. Don't use these frameworks to reflect upon your digital skills (i.e., screencasting, blogging, using augmented reality) but instead reflect upon your digital instructional practices (i.e., using screencasting to differentiate for students, blogging to cultivate stronger student voice, using augmented reality to add another perspective to learning).

2. **Reflect, don't evaluate.** While it is clear that the goal in both of these tools is to move up the scale, the SAMR and TIM frameworks should be used as a guide to reflect upon practice—not to evaluate it. Innovation is about taking risks and getting out of your comfort zone. This is not an area that can be evaluated. Either you are taking risks or you're not. To evaluate

is to insinuate that failure is a bad thing—and in risk taking, failure is part and parcel to the process (in Chapter 5, we will explore this concept in more depth). It's reflection that's most important when trying to make impactful change.

SETTING A COURSE FOR INNOVATION

Innovation is an ambiguous and daunting goal. Despite the fact that there are many ways to unpack this word and interpret it, there is one constant we can all agree on—we want the outcome to be better than what we started with. I use the phrase *Innovation Island* a few times throughout the book because it's catchy and I like a good alliteration. However, as you pursue innovation—a place where *different* and *better* coexist—you'll find that it's not stationary. It's a constantly moving target, making it difficult to plot a trajectory. Consider it one of those haunting floating islands from myths long ago; your goal is to sail through the mist and find it.

No big deal, right? Just find a mythical island called Innovation using your magical boat made of digital tools and do all of it while navigating around the many obstacles along the way. How are you supposed to do this? Well, it's easier to recognize *different* and *better* when you know what is better. It is also easier to achieve grander levels of *better* when we first start small. So, to help us measure a tangible improvement and get you started on your journey, this book starts with you—your needs and your challenges—before pushing out into deeper waters. In the next chapter, we will begin to dig into these challenges and set up a process to begin your edventure.

chapter 2

PROBLEM-BASED LEARNING

It's Not Just for Kids

OK, we've set a course toward Innovation Island. Now how do we get there?

It's one thing to internalize the concept of innovation and yet another thing entirely to understand the route to get there. So how does one who wants to transform learning but has no idea where to start get started? Well, we established in the previous chapter that innovation is about changing things for the better. Therefore, we need to know—what are we changing and what about it needs to be improved? Rather than starting with grandiose ideas involving virtual reality, redefined school day schedules, and transformed classroom spaces, it helps to start small. And to start small, we go to a big source: your problems.

This is something teachers around the globe have in common—a list of problems wider and deeper than the ocean itself. We share them over our coffees while supervising morning entry and dismissal and in the rare occasions when we have time to eat lunch together. We lament to our partners and families about "if only." So what would you do if you had a magic wand and could somehow finally address one of these nagging problems? Would that make your educational life different and better?

You might have heard of—or utilized—problem-based learning (PBL) as a strategy for teaching students. It's the method of centering a unit of study on a problem and designing all learning activities and outcomes around solving this problem. It gives your study a purpose and does wonders for student engagement. My experience using PBL in my classroom was so successful that when I began to work with adult learners (i.e., my fellow teachers), I decided to try this out with them as well.

Problem-based innovation (PBI) maps out your journey by first identifying existing problems of practice so as to determine a solution-based action plan. It roots itself in your personal needs and intrinsically builds that oh-so-needed buy-in. Think about it—when you are given another goal to tackle or strategy to learn, regardless of how much you believe in the philosophy, it's difficult to give it your all when it's one more thing on top of the many problems that are already plaguing you.

This isn't to say that you haven't already tried to solve these problems. PBI invites you to look at it from a different angle with the help of a different set of tools. If you can use these new tools and strategies to first address these problems, it can have a twofold positive effect: demonstrating the impact of technology on real problems and clearing your plate rather than adding to it. Once one of your challenges has been addressed, you'll have renewed mental and emotional space to dig into taking risks and trying new things.

As time goes on and these initial problems are successfully addressed, you will be better prepared to sail further toward your ultimate destination and try some of those newfangled ideas. So to get started on your PBI adventure, let's first identify your most plaguing problems, understand them, and come up with a route to circumvent them.

TEACHER INNOVATION EXPLORATION PLAN: AN INDIVIDUALIZED EDUCATION PROGRAM FOR TEACHERS

Framing the PBI experience isn't always an easy task for a busy teacher. As such, I've developed a template to scaffold the process: the Teacher Innovation Exploration Plan or TIEP. Adapted from the idea of a student Individualized Education Program (IEP), the TIEP focuses your PBI around a selected problem of practice and then guides you in a scaffolded plan to meet this challenge. You can find two versions of an interactive TIEP template on the companion website, one for individual use (Figure 2.1) and one to use with or as a coach (Figure 2.2). Scan QR Code 2 to visit the page.

QR Code 2

IDENTIFYING THE PROBLEM OF PRACTICE

To begin with your TIEP, you first need to identify what specific issues are weighing you down. One way I like to do this is an activity I call the "Gripe Jam."

I have teachers sit at large tables or individual desks with plenty of room to spread out. After giving everyone a stack of sticky notes, I let the teachers know that we're about to engage in a Gripe Jam. (Note: While I did this with a whole group during a meeting, you can certainly try it yourself with a stack of sticky notes at your desk or kitchen table.)

FIGURE 2.1 TIEP Teacher Version (Blank)

Teacher Innovation Exploration Plan (TIEP)

PROBLEM OF PRACTICE

Problem Description (be as detailed as possible)

Past Solutions

What you've already tried	What worked	What didn't work

NEW SOLUTION

New Solution	
What you need to accomplish this	Support you need (and from whom)

Action Plan

Action Item	Step-by-Step to Do List	Due Date	Needs / Notes / Reflection

FINAL REFLECTION

What worked	What didn't work
What will you do differently next time?	

FIGURE 2.2 TIEP Coaching Version (Blank)

Teacher Innovation Exploration Plan (TIEP)—Coaching Version

PROBLEM OF PRACTICE

Problem Description (be as detailed as possible)

Past Solutions

What you've already tried	What worked	What didn't work

NEW SOLUTION

New Solution	
What you need to accomplish this	**Support you need (and from whom)**

Action Plan / Coaching Notes

Action Item	Meeting Notes	Due Date	Next Steps (Coach)	Next Steps (Teacher)

FINAL REFLECTION

What worked	What didn't work
What will you do differently next time?	

I then ask the teachers to think about all of the challenges they face throughout their educational lives. As they do, they should write each problem on a sticky note. They are to follow two guidelines while doing so:

- One problem per sticky note
- No problem is too big or small (don't sort your problems yet, just get them all down on paper)

To help the teachers bring to mind problems they may face, I give them situations to imagine, one at a time:

- You just arrived at school.
- Your students are entering the classroom.
- You're teaching a whole-group lesson.
- You're teaching a small-group lesson.
- Your students are participating in group work.
- It's your planning period.
- It's lunch time.
- Your students just left for the day.
- You're sitting in professional development.
- It's Sunday night.
- You're grading work.
- You're in a staff meeting.
- It's the middle of the night and you can't sleep because . . .

Then I play the rock anthem "We're Not Gonna Take It," let them know that they have until the end of the song to write down any and all challenges they face in their classrooms, and let them go at it.

Once the song is over, they spread their notes out on their desk. This is a pretty simple idea: allowing yourself to gripe about problems. This happens unofficially every day in teachers' lounges, after school, and over dinner tables. However, the next part of the process is the important differentiator between staff room griping and a productive Gripe Jam.

After teachers finish their cathartic unloading of obstacles, they shake out the pile and try to categorize the complaints. They ask themselves a series of questions to analyze and sort the problems as follows (see Figures 2.3–2.7 for examples)

- How frustrating do you find these problems?
  (sort in a straight line from most frustrating to least frustrating, left to right)
- How many people does this problem affect?
  (move them up or down based on approximate number of people affected, keeping them in their horizontal order)
- Which of these problems are you most passionate in solving?
  (draw a circle around these notes)

FIGURE 2.3 Write Down All of Your Problems

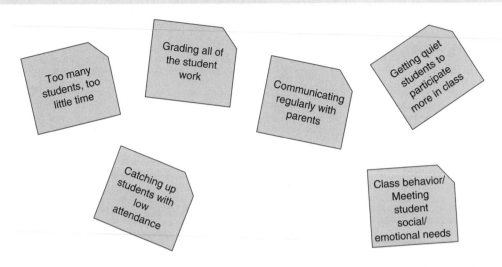

FIGURE 2.4 How Frustrating Do You Find These Problems?

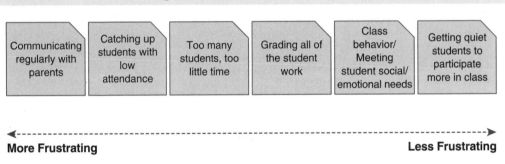

More Frustrating   **Less Frustrating**

FIGURE 2.5 How Many People Do These Problems Affect?

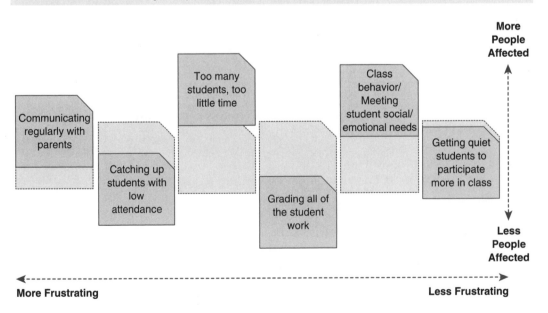

FIGURE 2.6   Which Problems Am I Most Passionate About Solving?

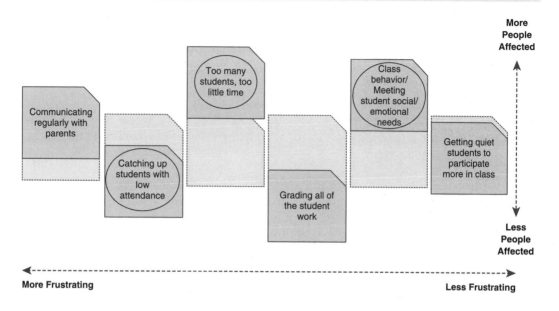

FIGURE 2.7   Focus Here to Start

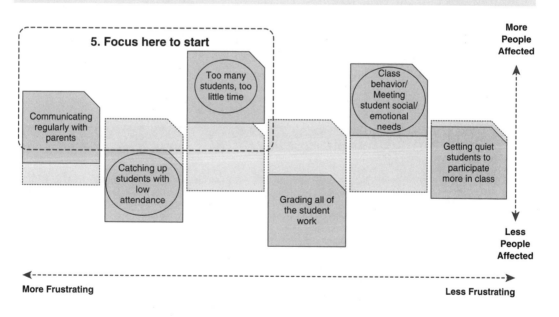

You can go through this Gripe Jam as a collaborative group or as an individual. If you decide to engage in this process as a group, an optional added activity is a gallery walk. Once the problems have been sorted and circled, everyone gets up and silently examines each other's Gripes. As participants circulate and review their colleagues' problems, they can leave notes regarding the following:

- Ideas to address a challenge
- Contact information to collaborate on a challenge
- Encouraging notes or a star to give a "yeah, me too" nod of agreement about a challenge

Upon returning to original workspaces, participants review notes left to them and update their sort based on what they saw on other tables and/or feedback given. I love to see the collective sigh that arises when colleagues see that they aren't alone in their struggles . . . and when they sometimes receive the gift of a collaborator who has volunteered to team up and attack that struggle together.

After teachers complete their sort (and the optional gallery walk), it's time to select a problem of practice. I ask them to begin by looking at the top left quadrant. These will be the problems that affect the most people and cause them the most frustration. Still, if they see a circled problem that they're passionate about solving but is located in another quadrant, they can certainly decide to start there. The most important thing is that you are excited and motivated by the challenge.

You should also start to ask yourself, can technology help me in solving this problem? The answer may be no, and that may be okay. It may be something you still want to take another look at and try to solve in a new way. Remember: Innovation is not contingent on technology. However, for the purpose of this book, try to select a problem that has the potential to be solved with technology. Not sure if it can be? That's what Part II of this book is for!

Choosing the Best Problem: What to Avoid

As I have mentioned already, when innovating in schools, tools are too often the focus. So when selecting a problem of practice, while you certainly want to think about how tech can be part of the solution, be sure it focuses on **pedagogy**, not tools. For many, the first challenge to come to mind is logistics, like finding the money to purchase devices, programs for devices, peripherals (cases, headphones, power stations), Wi-Fi, and so on. And yet, more and more schools are beginning to solve these initial problems only to realize that they now have piles of tech in classrooms and no plan on how to use them.

The second challenge often considered is simply taking out and using the devices each day. More and more digital learning programs are being created to take traditional workbooks and repackage them as animated activities. Yet, does simply digitizing instruction improve student learning? What opportunities does this provide that analog tools cannot? How are these opportunities better than before?

I would argue that these "adaptive" learning programs offering scores of word problems, video lessons, and multiple choice questions aren't truly providing improved opportunities for our students. Sure, they are different. Initially, they may be more engaging. But the novelty soon wears off for our kids as they realize they have been duped into a talking, dancing worksheet. We want to avoid making a change simply for the sake of being new or different. Therefore, as you select a challenge, be sure it focuses on **teaching** and **learning**. If you can solve that problem, you will be taking steps toward implementing changes that improve opportunities for your kids—and thus moving closer to true classroom innovation.

However you engage in the Gripe Jam, this process will help you identify a problem to solve. This problem will be the focal point around which you will build your TIEP, so it is important to take the time to find a good one.

DEFINING THE PROBLEM OF PRACTICE

Once you have selected a problem of practice and have added it to your TIEP, it's time to really get to know it. This problem is going to be the focus of your innovation efforts for the foreseeable future, so you want to make sure you truly understand all aspects of it.

First, write out a narrative of the challenge. Cite examples where it hinders your practice and explain what about it is frustrating. It helps to even write out times of day or days of the week that this problem is especially prevalent.

Next, list out any and all solutions to this problem that you have previously attempted. Talk to colleagues and see what they have tried. Be sure to list out what worked and didn't work for each attempted and discarded idea. It's important to try to identify *why* previous attempts didn't work so as to determine what facets of those attempts *did* work. Oftentimes it wasn't the solution as a whole that wasn't successful but aspects of it. Those pieces are the bright spots you'll want to focus on as you build a new and improved approach.

If you haven't attempted to solve this problem in the past, you can still list out potential solutions you had considered but dismissed before attempting. Why didn't you go for it—a lack of time? A perceived obstacle? Lack of resources? Write these out as well.

STEPPING UP TO A SOLUTION

After you've spent some time getting familiar with your problem, it's time to explore various ideas to address them. This is where Part II of this book comes into play. Look at the various categories of problems and see if you can find one that's similar to yours—or perhaps I have written about your very problem itself (#nailedit)! For each problem, I offer some suggestions to try out. I don't want to call them solutions quite yet—that's for you to decide pending their success in your situation.

As you read through the suggestions, ask yourself which seems to fit your style, situation, and need the best. Of course, you may need to tinker with the strategy to personalize it to your setting. There may be more than one suggestion you'd like to try but pick one to start; you can always iterate and come back to this book to try an alternate approach.

Once you've found a potential solution, it's time to set up your step-by-step action plan. As you begin, keep the following five tips in mind:

1. *Take small bites.* Remember, it's important to take small bites. Some of the suggestions offered in this book are simple while others are quite complex. In any case, you want to outline specific action steps to implement this new idea in your classroom or school. So instead of writing down "get parent permission for students to use Twitter," break this down into smaller steps: (1) write informational letter to parents, (2) schedule parent info meeting, (3) create permission slips, (4) offer permission slips at meeting, (5) send home permission slips with students whose parents did not attend meeting, and so on. This will increase your chance of completing the tasks and also help you to foresee any issues and understand what resources—be it time, space, or physical materials—you need to be successful.

2. *Hold yourself accountable.* Once you have a set list of tasks chunked into small and concrete steps, set due dates for each. The template also allows for a section to reflect on each step after it has been completed: What worked? What didn't? Is there still work to be done to complete this step? It helps to not only set the due dates on the TIEP but also on whatever planning calendar you use. Be it a high-tech digital calendar on your phone or computer or a paper-and-pencil planner, note these dates and even schedule periods of time to work on your action plan steps.

3. *Know what you need.* As you are creating your action steps, remember that educating students is a team effort. Asking for help is an important step in improving your practice. Be sure to outline what support you need, be it permission from parents, support from administration, or access to learning spaces or tools. Be sure to note who you're requesting support from and add this as an action step. (Tip: Add an action step to send follow-up requests, as oftentimes initial e-mails go unnoticed in busy school environments.)

4. *Focus on the problem, not the strategy.* While this may seem negative, it's an important mindset. As you get into the problem-solving process, it's easy to lose sight of the forest through the trees. By this

I mean you may become overly focused on the nuances of the approach and forget the problem you're trying to address. It can become about the tool or the workflow rather than trying to solve the problem. If the approach isn't working, feel free to toss parts of it out the window and retool the concept midstream.

5. *Celebrate small wins.* When tackling a problem, remind yourself to stop and reflect on what successes you achieve along the way. Too often, we wait to celebrate until the whole battle has been won, but emotionally, you may need more frequent reinforcement. If a particular part of your idea or day went well, take it for what it is—a win.

For an example of a completed action plan, see Figure 2.8.

FIGURE 2.8 Example of Teacher Innovation Explorer Plan (TIEP)

Teacher Innovation Exploration Plan (TIEP)

PROBLEM OF PRACTICE

Problem Description (be as detailed as possible)
I spend all of my time grading student work! I teach four sections of 6th grade math and I feel like each night, I am grading 122 homework sheets, exit tickets, classroom activities and/or tests. I hate it! I'm constantly buried in this paperwork.

Past Solutions

What you've already tried	What worked	What didn't work
Assigning less centers activity work.	There was less grading.	The students weren't as accountable for what they did in the centers.
Having students peer-grade their work.	Nothing.	I had to create an answer key and then the grading was superficial—they didn't give the same feedback I would have or they didn't understand the concept itself enough to help their peers. I ended up re-grading everything. I think if I had more time to teach them to give good feedback, they could do this for some activities, but for these assignments my students needed more in depth feedback.
Waiting to do all grading once a week.	It made me less stressed for four days—until I got to the grading day.	The day I had to do all the grading was a nightmare. Also, my students had to wait a week to get feedback.

(Continued)

FIGURE 2.8 (Continued)

NEW SOLUTION

New Solution
Using Google Forms and Google Sheets to grade student work

What you need to accomplish this	Support you need (and from whom)
<ul><li>Google Form</li><li>Google Sheet</li><li>Flubaroo</li><li>Conditional Formatting</li></ul>	<ul><li>Learn how to make a Form (YouTube).</li><li>Learn how to use Sheets (YouTube).</li><li>Learn how to use Flubaroo (YouTube).</li><li>Learn how to do Conditional Formatting (YouTube).</li></ul>

Action Plan

Action Item	Step-by-Step to Do List	Due Date	Needs / Notes / Reflection
Learn skills.	1. Set aside time to watch YouTube videos. 2. Watch videos. 3. Practice new skills.	11/1	https://www.youtube.com/watch?v=_3oJu91 KQV4 https://www.youtube.com/watch?v=U06W3 H_iDho
Create new activity formative assessments using forms.	1. Create Google Forms for students to submit "exit ticket" answers for each class. 2. Use Flubaroo to grade it. 3. Try this for a few lessons.	11/10	Going to use for Unit 5—hopefully first few lessons. Will keep trying if it works
Try creating multiple forms to make differentiated assessments.	1. Create three versions of the same assessment using three different forms. 2. Use Flubaroo to grade it. 3. Maybe put forms on a class website?	12/1	Reflection—this was really easy! Used a video on branching forms and actually made the differentiated questions part of the same form.
Try making a summative assessment on a form.	1. Create a final exam on the form. 2. See how to embed images. 3. Figure out how to mix order of questions to prevent cheating. 4. Make sure students know how to use form well.	12/10	Reflection—easy to add images as the teacher to the question, but students couldn't really show work. I had them show their work on a separate sheet of paper and turn that in. I still had to do some hand-grading, but it was less than normal.
See if form data are easier to enter into grade book.	1. Take spreadsheet data and put into grade book. 2. Take hand-graded work to put into grade book. 3. See if it is easier, same, or more challenging.	12/12	Reflection—It was easier with spreadsheet. I could sort their names in alpha order.

What worked	What didn't work
Saved lots of time on grading!	Showing work couldn't be done digitally this way.
Immediate differentiation in quizzes was really cool.	Long response answers couldn't be graded.
Students liked getting the feedback so quickly.	Getting the the form was tricky—had to make a class website to make it easier.
What will you do differently next time?	
Try to see if another method lets students input images. I heard there is something that lets you do this in a form. I have to do some more searching.	

CRITICAL FRIENDS

Asking for support from a variety of colleagues can be invaluable, and it can help to have a steady go-to person who knows your situation and is ready to hear new ideas and give feedback—someone who will keep you on track and make sure you stay the course in pursuing your TIEP. This is your Critical Friend.

More often than not, your Critical Friend is someone in a parallel position to yours—a fellow classroom teacher or, if you're a coach/administrator, someone with a similar set of duties. First, familiarize this person with your problem of practice—or, if possible—involve them in the Gripe Jam to determine the problem. Walk through your TIEP action plan and your progress to solve the problem. Schedule regular check-ins with this person—e-mails, phone calls, video conference calls, or in-person meetings. Ideally, this person is also embarking on an edventure themselves, so you can return the favor by being their Critical Friend as well!

Some tips for choosing a Critical Friend:

- Choose someone with whom you have a trusting relationship.
- Choose someone who you can meet with regularly, either in-person or via phone call or video chat.
- Choose someone who understands your situation and role.

Some ideas for getting started with your Critical Friend:

- Involve them in the Gripe Jam, if possible, or debrief the process afterward.
- Walk through your problem of practice with your Critical Friend and make sure he or she understands it as well as you do.

- Schedule out at least one month of check-in meetings at beginning. This will hold you to a schedule and help you stay accountable for digging into your TIEP.
- Set up norms about how you want to receive feedback and how you will work together.

Once you've set up your TIEP and mapped out a course for your problem-based journey, it's time to prepare your copilots in this adventure: your students. In the next chapter, I'll discuss some tips and tricks for getting them on board.

chapter 3

GETTING YOUR STUDENTS READY

Once you've determined your problem of practice and scoped out your Teacher Innovation Exploration Plan (TIEP), your students need to be prepared for the journey. They should feel like they are a part of this edventure as copilots rather than conscripted sailors. Involve them in charting the course from the beginning and equip them with what they'll need to be successful along the way.

The two main skills to build as you set sail are

- how to sail your new ships (i.e., use digital tools effectively) and
- how to stay safe on the sea (i.e., digital citizenship).

In this chapter, we will explore these points and ideas for steering your students in the right direction.

LEARNING TO SAIL: STUDENT INNOVATION TEAMS

Oftentimes, when I first sit down with a teacher at the beginning of her innovation journey, she laments, "I'm really most worried about my students knowing more about these [fill-in-the-blank tech tool] than I do." I always respond, "Good! Use them to help you!" Many students love opportunities for leadership. I remember having kids fight over who gets to be the line leader, chair stacker, lunch monitor—when really all they were doing was helping me do my job. Even older students enjoy a bit of responsibility. Oftentimes, our high school students would loiter in the library before/after school or on free periods, looking for odd jobs to do. When introducing digital tools to your classroom, use this same concept to your advantage.

For each digitally outfitted classroom, I suggest creating a student tech leadership team to help teach and support tech use. You can call this whatever you want: Apple Genius Bar (for iOS classrooms), iLeaders, Tech Titans, and so on. I called my group the Student Innovation Team, SIT for short. The group laughed at the acronym as they said, "We may be called SIT but we never actually get to do that—we're always on the go!"

Regardless of the name, it makes sense to build a team with enough students for a minimum 6:1 student–leader ratio. This allows for small-group support when rolling out new tech or complex digital workflows. I remember trying to teach my students a new app or program and directing them to "click the green button." Immediately I would hear a chorus of "I don't see a green button!" "My button is red!" "What did you say?" and "My iPad is broken!" I would then run around the classroom in a mad dash to respond and remedy these complaints. Once I had established my student leadership team (see Figure 3.1), I was able to calmly give the direction and all subsequent issues were immediately handled by the student leader stationed at each table or desk pod. I could circulate and support where needed, but for the most part, all problems were quickly and easily addressed.

Student leadership teams should be volunteer based to ensure buy-in. One way to build buy-in is making it application based. Teachers ask their students to apply for these positions in a similar manner to applying for a real job—by filling out an application and sitting for an interview. When K–2 classrooms want to use this model, the teachers ask students to draw a series of three pictures for their application: one picture of a time they acted like a leader, one picture of a time they solved a problem, and one picture of how they envision themselves in this job. Once the teams are established, teachers can even involve existing members to review new student leader applications.

FIGURE 3.1 Student Leadership Teams

After the students apply for the job and are selected, they are trained on how to be successful student leaders. As part of this training, the student leaders learn three golden rules by which they must abide:

1. Don't touch.
2. Go slow.
3. Be kind.

Don't Touch

Too often when someone asks for tech help, the person whose help was solicited simply takes the device and solves the problem for him. Although this fixes the problem in the moment, there is no learning for future problem solving. As such, we teach our student leaders to keep their hands behind their backs and lean in when supporting their peers. This stance helps the student stay focused on their peers and prevents succumbing to the desire to do it for them.

Go Slow

Usually the students who apply for these leadership teams are those that are quick on their feet—the first to finish their work, outgoing, and fast paced. While this makes them well-adapted to picking up tech concepts, it doesn't necessarily mean they have the patience to explain these concepts to their peers. I teach our student tech leaders to take it slow when explaining a process that they may deem simple to someone else. I ask them to practice breaking it down into the smallest steps they can think of and to count to three in their heads before giving the next step. The younger students actually count aloud, while the older students make this a mental routine. This wait time allows the other student to use this time to process the direction and successfully carry it out. My students teased me all the time that I talk too fast in class, so they even came up with the phrase "Oh no, you're going all Magiera on her" as a warning to slow down and count between steps.

Be Kind

Another common personality trait of our student leaders is difficulty empathizing with their peers' frustration. When I first began using student tech teams in our classes, I noticed that they quickly lost patience with those they were trying to support and their language bordered on unkind. Phrases like "Ugh, why are you so slow?" or "Oh geez, I can't believe you can't do that" were heard all too often. So during our initial student leadership training, the third golden rule we instill is kindness. We remind our students to envision how their teachers speak to them when they are frustrated and to model the same patient and kind language when working with their colleagues.

After they learn the three golden rules, the student leaders begin to meet on a regular basis to preview and practice tech tools and strategies. Depending on your particular situation, this could be before school, during a lunch period, or after school. The students get early access to new programs, apps, or strategies the class will soon be utilizing and have time to learn how they work, troubleshoot potential problems, and practice explaining their use to one another.

I've even seen this become a formal class or period during the day for middle school and high school students. These tech leadership groups go as far as to repair devices, give tutorials, and generally act as a tech help desk. They are able to help their peers as well as their teachers and school staff. Truly powerful examples of this push students even further to build apps or programs to solve school problems. In one of our schools, a student built a spreadsheet program to help with scheduling throughout the day while another created an app to help with dismissal safety.

These groups can even be pilot groups for potential tools or ideas that need vetting. I often had students try out apps I found and write reviews on them before I wrote them into our lessons. They would blog their reactions and even offer feedback to the developers themselves. See the following text box for one story about what transpired after my student blogged his reaction to a popular iOS app.

Student leadership groups are a useful way to instill a sense of student agency and empowerment into your classroom and school. It sends a message that this journey toward innovation and risk taking is a team effort between you and the class and creates powerful student buy-in. If you desire more structure and support in building your team, there are programs and web-based curricula such as Mouse Squad (http://mousesquad.org) that help you train and support students to take on these leadership roles.

In September of 2011, my student leaders were reviewing various annotation and screencasting apps (apps that allow you to handwrite over PDFs, blank screens, and other backgrounds). One in particular was a newer app called Explain Everything. One of my fifth graders, Kaleb, wrote the following review:

> "I dislike the eraser, the movement, the buttons on the side, and other things I don't know the name of. When you zoom in, it messes up your whole thing because all the pieces of my writing move around for no reason. It is really hard to erase because sometimes you don't get to erase things after a while. I hate it and I never want to use it again. I like noterize or newannotate better."

I posted his review to my blog and within a few weeks, I received an e-mail from Reshan Richards, the cocreator of Explain Everything. In it, he explained some of the features Kaleb had been frustrated with but also said the following:

> *"Please thank your students for their honest feedback! I am so sorry that they had trouble and were frustrated. With so many apps out there, it's all about finding the right tool for the intended learning outcome.*
>
> *Another idea that I wanted to offer you was if you, your students, or these two kids wanted to do a Skype chat with me one day and tell me about other things that they think would be good to improve, it could create an authentic opportunity for them to see how small the world can be and how powerful their words can be when their thoughts are published for an audience in a meaningful way."*

I was so impressed that an app developer wanted to hear from my class! We worked with their families to get permission for the video chat, set it up, and connected the students with Reshan. Kaleb proceeded to break down his feedback, explaining what worked for him, what didn't, and why. Reshan was incredibly engaged with the students, asking questions, giving clear answers, and thanking them earnestly for their thoughts. As the chat ended, I thought that was it (see Figure 3.2).

FIGURE 3.2 Explain Everything

 Explain Everything @explainevrythng · 19 Oct 2011
Had a great time skyping with the students of @MsMagiera! They helped find a bug and also suggested some great feature updates!

However, a few months later, Reshan reached back out again to let me know that thanks to Kaleb, he had reworked some of the features of his app. He said to let them know that they were now "app developers." I did and the looks on their faces when I told them were priceless. (They also asked if they were going to get a cut of the profits since they were now app developers.) All jokes aside, this was a powerful moment for the students. They were given a chance to be heard and given credit when their ideas made a difference. They knew this and it made a difference to them. In fact, in Kaleb's end-of-the-year video journal, he said, "I feel powerful because I was talking to this grown up and I told this grown up what to do to make the iPad App better. And that . . . changed my life."

QR Code 3

As an aside, Explain Everything has evolved and grown to be one of our favorite apps to use both in and out of the classroom—and not only because our students helped give feedback in these early stages. You can find resources on it at the companion website here (see QR Code 3).

STAYING SAFE ON THE
OPEN SEA: DIGITAL CITIZENSHIP

Equally as important as your students understanding how to use the technology is your students understanding how to stay safe when out on the digital sea. This means understanding what to keep private, the mark you're leaving out on the world, and how to respect others' work and self. For most, this is means building digital citizenship.

What Is Digital Citizenship?

Digital citizenship is a phrase that is becoming more and more commonplace in our classrooms as the access to digital tools increases. Some teachers balk at the time required to teach digital citizenship skills. Others teach one lesson at the beginning of the year and think it's done. Rather than thinking of digital citizenship as one more thing to get done on an ever-growing checklist, think of it as establishing norms at the beginning of each year. How do you let students know what is acceptable in your classroom environment? How do you explain the *why* for these expectations? And consider this: Do you really ever stop reinforcing these expectations throughout the year? Just as you prepare your students to be good citizens, so must we prepare our students to be good *digital* citizens.

So what do you need to teach when introducing digital citizenship? Essentially it is just that—being a positive citizen in the digital space. This means following many of the same norms we teach in our classrooms already. We just give them slightly different names:

1. respect for ourselves = data privacy and digital footprint
2. respect for others = cyberbullying and copyright

Respect for Ourselves

Respecting ourselves is a main piece of keeping safe online. To do so, our students should be familiarized with how to keep their information safe (data privacy) and the power of their digital footprint.

Data Privacy

There is an ever-growing concern about student data privacy. As I began to dig into more and more digital tools, I learned more about this topic. I found out about laws such as the Family Educational Rights and Privacy Act (FERPA) and Children's Online Privacy Protection Act (COPPA) that are designed to keep students' information private and learned that I should have been teaching them to be more cautious with their personal data.

FIGURE 3.3 FERPA and COPPA

	Family Educational Rights and Privacy Act (FERPA)	Children's Online Privacy Protection Act (COPPA)
Who It Applies to	Protects all students, including postsecondary students Schools are the responsible party.	Students under 13 years old
What Exactly It Is Protecting	Personally identifiable information The term includes, but is not limited to • the student's name; • the name of the student's parent or other family members; • the address of the student or student's family; • a personal identifier, such as the student's social security number, student number, or biometric record; • other indirect identifiers, such as the student's date of birth, student's place of birth, and mother's maiden name; • other information that, alone or in combination, is linked or linkable to a specific student that would allow a reasonable person in the school community, who does not have personal knowledge of the relevant circumstances, to identify the student with reasonable certainty; or • information requested by a person who the educational agency or institution reasonably believes knows the identity of the student to whom the education record relates.	Personal information including • first and last name; • a home or other physical address, including street name and name of a city or town; • online contact information; • a screen or user name that functions as online contact information; • a telephone number; • a social security number; • a persistent identifier that can be used to recognize a user over time and across different websites or online services; • a photograph, video, or audio file where such file contains a child's image or voice; • geolocation information sufficient to identify street name and name of a city or town; or • information concerning the child or the parents of that child that the operator collects online from the child and combines with an identifier described above.
The Gist— What the Law Says	Parents and guardians have the right to inspect and review their student's records as well as the right to amend inaccurate records. They also have the right to first consent before student records are shared with third parties (with some exceptions, i.e., school officials, financial aid institutions, judicial orders, health/safety emergencies).	Websites cannot collect personal information from children under 13 without parental permission. Additionally, information collected by websites cannot be sold or given to third parties. However, schools can consent on behalf of a parent when using a website for educational purposes. When acting as the consenting party, schools should be cautious to read website privacy policies to ensure they comply with COPPA.

(Continued)

FIGURE 3.3 (Continued)

	Family Educational Rights and Privacy Act (FERPA)	Children's Online Privacy Protection Act (COPPA)
Why This Is Important	Parents have a right to know who is seeing their student's data and what the data say about their child and to object if there are clear inaccuracies.	Websites collecting information may share this with advertisers who may target the student or share it with unscrupulous third parties. Student personal information is part of their growing digital footprint and online identity. There is concern of companies tracking children at a young age without parental consent.
Tips for Complying	Be sure not to leave student records out in public places or keep your digital gradebook open and unattended. If you get a student record request, reach out to your administration for support to comply.	Check the privacy policies of websites to check: • Do they explicitly say they comply with COPPA? (Desired response: Yes) • Do they explicitly say that students under 13 cannot use this site? (Desired Response: No. Watch out for this one! Websites often cover themselves legally by adding a line to their privacy policy that says users must be 13 or older. If you teach K–8 students, this may mean your students cannot use this tool.) • Are you able to request that all student information be deleted at any time? (Desired response: Yes) If using a website that collects personal information from students, be sure to let parents know. You can do this by sending home a letter or posting a list of programs used in your classroom on your class website—or both! Some districts have a list of preapproved programs. Check with your curriculum or technology teams to see if this list exists. Help your students become guardians over their own data! See below for some ideas and strategies.

This simply was not something that was covered in my educational prep classes nor something widely discussed at staff meetings. I found the laws daunting and complex—I was unsure of what applied to me, what applied to my administration, and what, if anything, I was responsible for doing. Now that I'm a district administrator, I've seen the need for data privacy at all levels. For a quick crash course on these two important laws, see Figure 3.3. (For more information, see the Privacy Toolkit created by the Consortium for School Networking at http://cosn.org/privacy.)

After I familiarized myself with the importance of data privacy, I began to educate my students about the importance as well. While COPPA applies directly to my younger students, I knew that it was important for all of my students, regardless of age, to understand how and why they needed to keep data private.

This began on a small scale for me in the classroom around protecting student passwords. In the past, my class would use one another to practice memorizing their passwords by playing games or asking a friend to help them login. They would save their passwords on pieces of paper taped to notebooks, where anyone could find them. Inevitably, a few kids with less-than-pure intentions used their peers' passwords to delete or modify work or even to send incriminating messages to each other and staff members.

We began by discussing the importance of account privacy and safety. We brainstormed potential issues for data being compromised, from identity theft to becoming the target of marketing. We then came up with better solutions for learning and internalizing secure information. In the case of passwords, I had two main methods: For younger students, I passed out passwords taped to the inside of file folders. I would give them to students to practice password memorization each day and then collect them so they wouldn't be out in the open. For older students, I simply emphasized the need to keep them secure. In some cases, I shared passwords with parents directly so they could support at-home memorization and logins.

Regardless of age, I created cards to help students stop and ask before giving out certain information to digital strangers (i.e., websites, people online, or apps). They referenced these cards and learned to be better guardians of their own personal data (see Figure 3.4).

Digital Footprint

As your students post more and more information online—personal photos and videos, student work, social media posts—it develops into their digital footprint. In an age where more and more people can be Googled and where employers are combing through popular social media sites before offering jobs, it's important that our students understand the impact their choices have on their present and future.

FIGURE 3.4 Personal Data List

CAUTION:
Stop and ask your teacher or parent before sharing any of the following information!

❑ Name
❑ Phone number
❑ Address
❑ Username
❑ Password
❑ School
❑ Name of your family members
❑ Birthday
❑ Email address
❑ Photo or video of you

In fact, many are no longer calling this a *digital footprint* but rather a *digital tattoo*. After all, a footprint can be washed away with the daily tides, but a tattoo is permanent—difficult and painful to remove. This metaphor alone has helped some of my students take pause when posting something online. So when deciding to add something to their digital tattoo, we prompt students to ask a few reflective questions:

• Would I be comfortable with my parents seeing this?
• Would I be comfortable with a stranger seeing this?
• Will I be proud of this in three years? (Note: I used to ask them if they'd be proud in 10 years, but my students couldn't think that far out.)

This is a good collaborative reflection activity. Have your students practice reflecting on various sample social media posts. Ask them to discuss pros and cons of word choice, media upload, and message. Prompt them to give hypothetical feedback to these individuals, then have them examine their own online activity.

If they are under 13 and not officially active in social media, it's still important to build this awareness. While we must acknowledge that it is far too easy for our students to fake a birthdate and create an account, we must also acknowledge that preparing our students ahead of time, even if they aren't defying social media age limits, can only help prepare them for the future.

Respect for Others

Cyberbullying

This is one of the most common concerns when introducing digital tools into the classroom. The concern that students will use these anonymity of a screen to send hurtful messages to one another is to be taken seriously. It's important that we teach students to communicate with respect for one another and to be upstanders when witnessing bullying.

There are many online resources to teach prevention and awareness of cyberbullying, but my personal favorite is Common Sense Media (http://common sensemedia.org). This site is broken down by age and provides an incredible wealth of tools to teach, prevent, and—if needed—respond to cyberbullying. There are even gamified courses students can move through that are suited to their age range. Additionally, this is a great site to share with families. An entire parents section provides a helpful and easy to use Q&A page with common at-home digital problems and responses for each. Simple and clear videos accompany many of these articles, providing student, parent, and teacher testimonies to help with building understanding.

Although this curriculum is great, it shouldn't stand on its own. Just as is the case when combating face-to-face bullying, the most powerful strategy is building strong relationships with and between your students. A strong classroom community trumps after school specials and gamified anti-bullying curriculum. In Chapter 8, I share various ideas to help build a positive classroom culture. Feel free to skip ahead to collect a few ideas before you set off on this journey.

Copyright

Respecting others' work is not as simple as avoiding obvious plagiarism (i.e., copy/pasting an article from the web and turning it in for an assignment). Even teachers struggle with this one—using "free" online music, videos, and images in class websites, videos, and slideshows. Students should learn that being a digital citizen means understanding when and how you can use someone else's work and how to properly give credit. Depending on their age, they should be familiarized with Creative Commons (see QR Code 3) and practice searching for open-source content to use in their projects (see Figure 3.5).

QR Code 3

http://creative commons.org/

Now that your students are equipped with the skills to sail their ships and be safe on the sea, it's time to prepare the ships themselves: our digital tools. These will be the vehicles that will take us to Innovation Island, so we need to make sure everything is right and ready. In the following chapter, we'll dig into this next step.

FIGURE 3.5 Creative Commons Cheat Sheet

Creative Commons is a nonprofit organization that supports sharing digital resources and products through free copyright licenses. It standardizes the way people can provide and search for permissions for creative work. Below are the 6 licenses offered:

Attribution: You can use and edit this work, even commercially as long as you give credit.

Attribution-Share Alike: You can use and edit this work, even commercially as long as you give credit and use the same CC license as the original work.

Attribution-NoDerivs: You can use this work, even commercially but you cannot edit it and you must give credit.

Attribution-NonCommercial: You can use this work and edit it, but you cannot use it commercially and you must give credit.

Attribution-NonCommercial-ShareAlike: You can use this work and edit it, but you cannot use it commercially, you must give credit, and use the same CC license as the original work.

Attribution-NonCommercial-NoDerivs: You can use this work, but you cannot edit it, use it commercially, and you must give credit.

chapter 4

GETTING YOUR MATERIALS READY

Now that you've got your students on board and your journey mapped out, it's time to ready your ships: your digital tools. How will you maintain all of these devices? You're already orchestrating a carefully choreographed dance every day in supporting the movements and materials of your students—now how will you manage adding digital tools to the mix? How will you handle powering them, syncing them, distributing them, troubleshooting them, and keeping track of them?!

In this chapter, I will share five pieces of advice I share with all of my colleagues who are powering up their classrooms with tech. Hopefully these tips will help you go digital without going nuts.

1. Let the students lead the way.
2. Build a management system.
3. Rewrite your supply list.
4. Tech is not a treat.
5. Less is more.

LET THE STUDENTS LEAD THE WAY

In the previous chapter, I discussed how to set up and support a student leadership team. This group will be pivotal in supporting their peers in how to navigate the programs, apps, and workflows using the devices, but it is also helpful in the physical management of the device themselves.

Some ideas for how this group can help include

- distributing devices;
- collecting, charging, and securing devices;
- cleaning devices;
- being log-out captains (ensuring every student has successfully logged out of his or her device before they leave for the day to maintain account security); and
- troubleshooting Wi-Fi/app issues.

Just as your students are leading their peers in the use of the devices, giving them these added responsibilities also help them lead in the proper care for the devices as well. Many junior high and high schools have even formalized this role as a class or volunteer job in their tech departments. Their student tech teams are the backbone of device support and maintenance in their buildings. In addition to providing leadership and problem-solving opportunities, these tech teams also help their student members move on to pursue career paths in technology. Scan QR Code 4 to visit the companion website and see examples of schools using this model.

QR Code 4

BUILD A MANAGEMENT SYSTEM

When students get new classroom tools—it doesn't matter whether they are math manipulatives, pipe cleaners, or an iPad—they immediately want to play with it. I learned a long time ago as a math teacher to give my kids time to get that out of their system before trying to be productive with the tools. So when my fourth and fifth graders got their iPads, I wasn't surprised that they wanted to take selfies, search for images of celebrities, and change their wallpaper background. The first few years, I spent an inordinate amount of time fussing at my students and trying to regulate this distraction. However, over time, I realized that I needed to let it go and turn these lemons into lemonade.

Rather than mandating that they couldn't touch those settings, I learned to make this an activity for their first day. I had kids start with their iPad number (they were each numbered according to their cart slot number, see Figure 4.1). Then they were able to personalize their number with images and messages that represented their personal and academic goals for the year. One girl hoped to join the track team and so she drew sneakers with wings. Another boy wanted to get all As so he drew a series of multicolored As in various fonts and sizes around his head. After the students had adorned their number with their hopes and dreams, we set these images as the iPad wallpaper. For those students who shared devices, they worked collaboratively on their wallpaper.

This not only created a positive way for the students to personalize their device, circumventing the desire to set less-than-school-appropriate wallpaper images, but it also made it much easier to keep track of whose device was whose.

We also adhered contact paper cut into various shapes onto the back of the devices—one shape per student group. This helped us identify the device even if it was powered off. It also helped organize the students quickly into learning groups based on shape: "Today all triangles and squares will begin posting their work" or "If your shape has an odd number of angles, please come to the rug for small group." For laptop-style devices, this was especially

FIGURE 4.1 iPad Numbers

helpful, as all teachers could identify devices from the back of the screen while they were in use.

Teachers who have a bring-your-own-device or take-home device model also face the challenge of the drained battery. How do you get your kids to bring fully charged devices to school? What do you do if they die during class?

Try creating a juice bar—a power station for your classroom. Ask for power strips in your school supply lists or add them to your own school shopping list and place them somewhere in your classroom. The trick is to put them somewhere less-than-enticing. The trap many teachers doing this fall into is that they go too far in making their juice bar an attractive and comfortable place to be. Unsurprisingly, more and more students start showing up to your classroom with low batteries. The juice bar should be placed somewhere in the classroom where kids don't want to sit, so it's a last-resort support rather than a destination to be desired.

In addition to numerating and cataloging, you'll also want to consider how they are accessing the device during the day. Are they out on their desks all day? Do they put them in the middle of the table or in their cubby when not being used? Most mobile devices purchased for educational use have a battery life that stands up well to the school day and so don't need to be charged mid-day.

FIGURE 4.2 Headphones and Tablets on Table

As such, consider keeping them out somewhere all day, not putting them back in the cart (see Figure 4.2). Doing so would sacrifice precious learning time and would also add to the wear and tear of the cart and devices.

REWRITE YOUR SUPPLY LIST

Now that you have digital tools, you'll need digital accessories. Rethink that list of spiral notebooks and three-ring binders. Consider asking students or parents to bring in materials that will help facilitate your tech-laden classroom. Here is a 21st-century supply list to start you off:

For Your Child

- Stylus (in a zipper bag, with student's name on it)
- Headphones (in the same bag as the stylus—please send an inexpensive over-ear model if possible as they will stay at school)
- Screen wipes

For the Class

- Antibacterial wipes
- Power strips

If families aren't able to send in these supplies, check your local dollar stores for headphones and consider making your own styluses. Below is a fun science activity that explores how touchscreens work and allows your students to harness the power of science to make their own styluses (Figure 4.3).

FIGURE 4.3 Making a Homemade Stylus

A Money Saving Science Experiment: Making a Homemade Stylus

As more of our students are using touchscreen devices, teachers are realizing there is an added cost in peripherals . . . i.e., apps, headphones and styluses. These costs can quickly add up, so finding simple low-cost solutions is quite helpful. Below is a quick way to create your own stylus with 3 household items in just a few seconds! Plus—BONUS—it makes an awesome science activity.

Materials:

- Q-Tips
- Small cup of salt water
- Tin foil

Steps:

1. Cut a strip of foil so it will wrap around all of the Q-Tip except the tip of the cotton.
2. Get your Q-Tip and wrap the foil around it so only the very tip of the cotton pokes out. The foil should be touching the cotton tip.
3. Wet the cotton tip (damp, not completely soaked) and use!

Optional: If you want a longer stylus handle, you can push it through the empty shell of a ballpoint pen! Just wrap the foil around the outside of the pen, and again make sure the foil touches the tip of the cotton.

Note: You do have to hold the stylus by the foil. You also will want to keep a wet sponge in the middle of your student tables so they can re-dampen their cotton—think like an old-school inkwell! (Ironic, no?)

Why does this work?

Most modern smartphones and tablets have something called capacitive touch screens. This means that they work because of a distortion in the screen's electrostatic field . . . basically it has to do with electrical current! While pure water is an insulator, adding even small amounts of salt can make it a conductor. Since humans are a bit salty;), we make decent conductors.

This is also why we have to take off our gloves when using our phones. Since the glove material is non-conductive, it won't "complete the circuit" and activate the screen sensors to operate the touch screen. The wet Q-Tip connected to the foil (a conductor) makes this stylus work. This is why the foil has to touch the salt-water soaked cotton and why you have to hold the foil and not just the bare plastic or paper handle.

TECH IS NOT A TREAT

So now that you have your devices organized, charged, and ready to go, what do you do if a student misuses it? That is, what is the appropriate response when a student is on the wrong app at the wrong time, downloads games to their device when they're supposed to be building a website, writes four-letter words on a class discussion board, or worse—engages in cyberbullying?

Many teachers go with the "you misuse it, you lose it" philosophy. We tell our students that the technology is a treat or privilege, and if they misuse it, we'll take it away. I myself was in this camp for quite some time. If my student did something inappropriate with their device, I had a stack of paperwork ready and waiting for them. They lost their iPad privilege for the day and had to earn it back. At first, it worked for me and seemed to work for the student. However, after some time, I realized that a few of my students were rarely using their devices. More and more they were losing this treat, and more and more they were getting accustomed to the paper version of our activity. I tried my best to keep the paper assignments as closely aligned as possible to what the rest of the class was doing digitally. And yet the more that technology allowed us to transform and improve learning opportunities, the wider the divide in paper and tech.

After a while, I realized that this consequence was hurting the students more than providing social-emotional instruction. Instead of being a reflective activity to teach the child the value of technology, I was depriving them of authentic learning opportunities and reinforcing their negative behavior. After a few instances of losing iPad privileges, certain students decided to disavow any desire to use the devices for classroom activities. When they were allowed to use them, they saw them as a treat, not as a learning tool. They were more inclined to play or simply pretend they didn't want to use it at all. In the end, I had succeeded only in teaching my students that our technology was a reward, not an essential vehicle for our learning or exploration.

Now as I work with teachers, I urge them to see technology as a foundational part of their instruction. They are challenged to unearth their problems of practice, and together we investigate how technology can alleviate these issues. In our highest-functioning 1:1 classrooms, the technology is invisible, a natural part of a transformed classroom—as ubiquitous as a pencil in many other rooms. So in this setting, how can we respond to student misuse by taking away this key learning tool?

To put it another way, if a student uses a pencil to write inappropriate phrases in the back of a math book, would you respond by taking away their math book privileges? Probably not . . . can you imagine if that got out? "Quick, to get out of math work, all you have to do is write inappropriate messages in the book! Wooo!" No, instead of revoking an essential learning tool for this misuse, we try to find instructional consequences that help students in making better choices in the future. So why should this be any different for technology?

In place of the "misuse it, you lose it" mindset, I implore teachers to treat their tech as they would any other essential learning tool. Yes, this is a much more powerful tool than a pencil or book. But should a student falter, don't take it away. Allow them to continue using it, but apply the same standards and consequences you'd give should they misuse any other essential learning tool—their pencil, book, desk, or chair. Also, proactively support students in understanding how to make good choices through scaffolding, goal setting, and clear expectations. We've taken on this new frame of mind in many of our classrooms and we're seeing tangible results. The students have greater respect for their digital learning tools and, most importantly, a greater access to opportunity.

If ultimately a student has a disability or focus issue and cannot immediately make positive use of the freedom a digital tool provides, consider scaffolding responsibility back in. Taking the tool away completely or indefinitely isn't a viable option, but temporarily restricting access with a clear understanding of how a student can earn more freedom may be useful. I've built out digital citizenship support plan to help teachers troubleshoot misconduct and respond with the ultimate intention of teaching a student to self-regulate him or herself. See the text box for more information.

Tier 1 Support (Start Here)

(1) Teacher reviews the Acceptable Use Policy and Digital Citizenship Agreement with the student and parent.

(2) Teacher utilizes Common Sense Media resources on digital citizenship with the student/class.

Tier 2 Support

(1) Teacher will convene a digital citizenship support team (i.e., teacher, innovation advocate, student, parents, and, if applicable, special education coordinator) to create a custom digital citizenship support plan.

(2) Support team will meet to develop and agree upon the following:

(a) Digital citizenship support plan

(b) Timeline for support

(c) Incentives

(d) Consequences

(Continued)

(Continued)

    (3) Teacher and student will carry out the support plan for the given timeline.

        (a) If successful, student will end plan and go back to Tier 1.

        (b) If unsuccessful, student will progress to Tier 3.

Tier 3 Support

    (1) After unsuccessful trial of Tier 2 support, the support team (with the addition of a school administrator) will meet to review lack of success and next steps.

    (2) The teacher will work with innovation advocate and tech team to explore digital restriction options for devices. Once digital restrictions are determined, the following will be determined:

        (a) a timeline for use,

        (b) a measure or process for students to earn back digital trust, and

        (c) a collaboration/communication plan between the school and the family.

    (3) If the student is successful in earning back trust according to the agreed-upon timeline and measures, they will move back down to Tier 2. If not, the student will continue on Tier 3 support and measures/timeline will be reevaluated by the support team.

LESS IS MORE

Another question I am often asked is, "What are the top apps to buy for [math, reading, writing, science, social science, etc.]?" My response is always, no matter the content in question: creation apps.

What do I mean by this?

I've found that often teachers get hung up on the best math game app or the best phonics app. Truth be told, the most amazing fractions game, states facts quiz app, or phonics app can only be stretched so far—perhaps one or two units (admittedly a bit longer for a good phonics app in primary classes).

However, a good creation app . . . wow, those pay dividends.

So I leave you with this: Consider the bang for your buck as you purchase apps. Will that measurement app really be used all year? Do you really want to spend $1.99 x 32 devices to buy it? Or would you rather spend $0.00 x 32 devices for a creation app that will push your kids to higher levels of thinking throughout your school year? Consider it. . . .

chapter 5

FALLING IN LOVE WITH FAILURE

CALLING FORTH YOUR COURAGE

I started this book with a question: *Will you join me on an adventure?* I also warned: *We must be courageous.* To embark on any adventure—or edventure—bravery is key. You're leaving the safety of the known and sailing off into uncharted territory. It's okay to be a scared—change is scary. The call to innovation is daunting. If you're this deep into the book already, it seems like you've decided to answer that call, to take a risk and try something new. Still, it's good to acknowledge that *deciding* to take these risks is only the beginning. Actually stepping forward and *taking* the risk is another thing completely.

I remember when I first decided to shake up my own practice. I was watching Sir Ken Robinson's TED Talk "Do Schools Kill Creativity?" (Spoiler alert: His answer is *yes*.) As I listened to him speak, I had that *ah-ha* moment when I realized that I had lost that optimistic "kids can do anything, be anyone" attitude I had embodied when I was training to become a teacher. Big data, big testing, and big district-level requirements had quashed that focus and instead, I spent my days creating anchor charts and rubrics and drilling my students. As I sat and listened to Sir Ken preach to me via YouTube, I decided then and there to change my approach and reintroduce creativity back into my classroom. I would change everything tomorrow.

And yet tomorrow became the next day . . . and the next day . . . and the next day . . . until over a year between that decision and "tomorrow" had elapsed. You see, it wasn't that I didn't have the passion and drive to pursue a different philosophy of education; it was that I was scared. Scared I'd fail: fail at this endeavor, fail my annual review, and, ultimately, fail my students.

As teachers, we are hardwired to avoid failure. Fail is literally a four-letter word. Don't let your students fail the test. Don't let your students fail out of school. Don't let your school fail to achieve test score goals. Don't fail *or else*. Or else they'll close your school. Or else your students won't get into a good college or grow up to lead happy and successful lives. There is so much pressure put on the shoulders of educators *not to fail*.

As a result, we can be too hesitant to take risks in our own practice. The fear of failure can be the biggest enemy to true innovation. It paralyzes us and keeps us from embarking on our edventure. In the search for different and better opportunities for our students, risks must be part of the game—and with risks come failure. So here's the message we need to internalize both for our students and ourselves: Failure shouldn't be feared. In fact, it's integral to growth and improvement. Improvements are seldom won without risk. Changes come rarely without courage. So as educators, we need to call forth that courage to appreciate the inevitability of failure and the fortitude to overcome it.

FAILING FORWARD

Therefore, as you launch into your journey, know that failure is not only inevitable but also productive. My friend Ken Shelton, an educator from the LA area, always says that yes, *fail* is a four-letter word, but we should also think of it as an acronym—FAIL = First Attempt In Learning. I love this as an easy way to present failure to students and to yourself.

There are so many examples of how a series of failures ultimately resulted in success: Edison's lightbulb, the Wright brothers' flying machine, and Churchill's quest for public office are just a few. In all of these stories, someone set off on a mission, took a risk, and failed multiple times but persevered until the goal was achieved. This is powerful message for our students but also for us as educators.

However, while the stories above teach us not to shy away from taking risks for fear of failure, the bigger lesson is to persevere and use any failures to inform future attempts. We must be constantly asking ourselves, "What did I learn from that failure and what will I do differently next time?" After all, Edison, Churchill, and the Wright brothers didn't simply take a risk, fail, and then give up. Each time they weren't successful, they learned something new from the attempt, improving and iterating subsequent tries until they reached their desired goal. So if FAIL is an acronym for First Attempt in Learning, then the *First* suggests a series of attempts, not a single one and done. Thus, I would add a second acronym to this concept—SAIL = Subsequent Attempts In Learning. After you FAIL, it's imperative that you SAIL. The initial failure (or string of failures) is a powerful learning opportunity. Use that learning and never give up after the initial botched attempt, but try again smarter and more informed from the previous experiences.

Now that we've established that failure isn't to be feared, we need to know where to expect it. There are three main places you will most likely encounter failure as you try out the ideas in this book: student failure, teacher failure, and system failure. Each has its own challenges, and each can be addressed differently. In this chapter, we will move through each with suggestions on how to optimize on the FAIL to the SAIL.

STUDENT FAILURE

As you begin to transform your classroom, you will be challenging your students to take on more agency, to become creators and change agents. As a result, they will face bigger obstacles and increased moments of frustration. Many of our kids struggle with this feeling, so it's important to build in a culture and climate that encourages risk taking and iteration and in which it feels safe to make mistakes.

The first step is to allow for more failure throughout the day. When we over-scaffold for our kids to ensure they are constantly experiencing success, never allowing them to feel moments of failure, we rob them of this opportunity to learn from mistakes and iterate. Surrounding them with scaffolds, anchor chart supports, and safety nets, they aren't given the chance to get frustrated and therefore be forced to creatively problem solve. This prevents them from being able to grow their stamina and resilience.

So audit your own practice. Is the scaffold or support you're providing necessary, or can they struggle a bit more to find their own way? For example, instead of giving them reference charts, can you give them strategies to seek out information on their own? Remember, if we give our students more opportunities to FAIL, they will have a chance to learn how to SAIL.

Another idea is to initiate a daily #FailFest. Note that this is a celebration of taking risks despite the fear of failure, not the failure itself. Consider it a version of laughing in the face of fear.

The way it works is that each day, you have students volunteer to share an example of a risk they took and a failure they encountered. After the student has shared, the class applauds her courage and she is awarded the #FailingForward ribbon. Then their classmates add to a #FailingForward online document (such as a Google Doc or other collaborative forum) with tips and ideas to avoid that failure in the future or improve on their next attempt. This document can be anything from a Google Doc to a blog or discussion forum. As the student uses these suggestions to make new attempts toward their goal, she can update this document to show future successes or failures.

Each step of this celebration is important. By inviting students to share their risks

> ### Recipe for a #FailFest
>
> #### 1. Share A Fail
> Share a story of risk and failure with your community.
>
> #### 2. Receive a #FailingForward badge
> Get the #FF badge to show you're a risk taker!
>
> #### 3. Solicit support from peers
> Get feedback from peers through a collaborative Google Doc or forum.
>
> #### 4. Try, try again and reflect!
> Use that feedback to iterate on the attempt and share a reflection with your community via the same doc / forum!

and failures, you make this process the norm. It helps promote a safe environment and allows students to expand their comfort zone.

In some ways, the second step is even more important. By asking their classmates to give feedback, it reminds the class that iteration is just as important as taking risks but also gives the student new ideas to try. A big problem with our discomfort of failure is that since we see it as taboo, we are reluctant to talk about it. If we don't talk about it, we can't get support and ideas for iterating on the initial attempt. Without this iteration, it's difficult for us to become better versions of ourselves.

To set the stage and model risk taking, I often am the featured FAIL for the first week. By doing this as the teacher, the students see that anyone can make a mistake and are quick to give me ideas for how I can be better. After a few days of sharing my FAILs and getting help, a few brave students are inevitably excited to get in front and share their stories.

TEACHER FAILURE

A #FailFest can be an impactful routine to have in the classroom but it is also a powerful routine for teachers. I've brought this to staff meetings and school setting as well, and it is successful for the same reasons it works for our students.

You might wonder, what are you to do if you don't have a community rallied behind you in a #FailFest or other routine? What should *you* do when you hit a pothole on your road toward innovation? There are many common reactions when educators face a failure:

- "I knew it wouldn't work anyway. Ugh. Boo to trying new things."
- "Well, I tried, but honestly I have to get this done and don't have time to retool it this time. . . . I'll try it again next year"
- "What didn't work? Let me rethink and regroup."

Obviously, the last option is the best next step, but *how* do you rethink and regroup? Here are some ideas to get support once your great idea doesn't quite pan out.

- **Reach out to your Critical Friend.** As we discussed in Chapter 1, it's important when working on your Teacher Innovation Exploration Plan (TIEP) to have someone who you can bounce ideas off of and get support from. This is a perfect chance for you to use this resource.
- **Make a success list.** It's likely that the entire endeavor wasn't a complete failure but rather that there were facets that were successful. Spend time trying to reevaluate the *entire* process and see what went well. Usually, you can rebuild the idea using those bright spots and learn from the mistakes.

- **Schedule time to iterate.** It's easy to say "I'll do it again . . . someday." Although you may not have time or opportunity to try it again immediately, set a date for when you *will* try it again. After all, without a chance to iterate, it's a waste of a perfectly good FAIL.

A Hot Mess . . . That One Time I Failed

In 2011, I was a new iPad 1:1 teacher with no idea what I was doing. I had begun to realize that I had to redefine my practice with a goal in mind and also knew I had to focus my efforts on these goals one at a time. The current problem I was attacking centered on differentiation during math centers. I wanted to find a way to work with more small groups in the short 25 minutes I had each day to do centers rotations. In Web searches and on social media outlets, I discovered the idea of *flipped classroom*. While giving videos to my students at home to watch on their own was not an option due to my kids' lack of technology, I knew I could adapt the idea to make it work.

I set out creating dozens of differentiated lessons using my computer's webcam. I set my computer on a desk in front of my dry erase board and taught short five-minute videos to it as if it was one of my students. It was pretty hilarious to my colleagues who would walk by and see me teaching to an empty room after school, but the payoff was worth my temporary insanity. I had a varied playlist of instructional and interactive videos ready for my students to use the next day! I set the computer to sync the videos to all of my iPads, switched off the lights, and called it a night.

The next morning, I was excited to try my new strategy. I told my students about the videos, showed them how to pull them up, and gave them each a personalized playlist on an index card so they knew which videos to watch. I pulled a small group to work with myself and settled in for the magic to happen.

Immediately, the room filled with peals of nervous laughter and snickering. I couldn't figure out what was so funny—were factors and prime numbers now hilarious? I walked over to a student's desk to find, to my intense horror, that instead of syncing my 12 videos to the devices, I'd instead somehow managed to upload the 2010 buddy comedy *Hot Tub Time Machine*.

I quickly gave panic-filled directions for all students to put their iPads back in the cart and took those few moments to think. What should I do? I was probably going to get fired for putting this movie on my fourth grader's iPads. I could wipe them and pretend it never happened and never take out the devices again. Or . . .

I owned up to it. I told my students what I had meant to sync to their devices and I said, "I made a mistake." I talked about my failure and what I would do differently (i.e., double-check my work—in this case, iTunes—to make sure I was syncing the

(Continued)

right videos). I talked about how, at first, I had wanted to pretend it didn't happen and to quit using the iPads (groans from students here) and instead, I realized that I could learn from my mistake.

Then I talked to my students about movies, media, and choices in entertainment. We talked about rating systems and why some videos are rated for all audiences and others should only be watched by minors with parental permission. This resulted in a debate about censorship and freedom of speech and how that related to movie ratings. All of this occurred in the 25 minutes we were supposed to be in math centers and, to be honest, was probably the most powerful moments of learning that week.

SYSTEM FAILURE

You just spent the past weekend/week/month preparing for an incredible digital activity and just as you're about to rally your students to this task, the Wi-Fi goes down/program glitches/logins don't work. Ack! And your principal is observing today! Ack Ack! What to do? Give up, obviously.

No! When facing system failure, know that there is really little you can do to prevent it. The fickle friend that is technology often gives us a scare when it's the most inconvenient. The best thing to do here is to be over-prepared. And by this, I don't mean making paper copies of all student assignments each time you craft a digital activity. Instead think about the activity itself: What are the salient pieces that are getting at student learning? If you're building toward a digital ecosystem in which the technology is *pushing* or *redefining* learning rather than replacing simple learning tools, this is even easier. While the activity won't be as powerful as the original plan you had utilizing the tech, it will maintain its original purpose.

Figure 5.1 shows some examples of how to pivot when a digital system goes down.

FIGURE 5.1 Fail Pivot Ideas

Digital Activity	Objective	Fail Pivot Ideas
Digital assessment (form, online quiz, clickers)	Assessing student knowledge / needs to inform future instruction / support	– Use a doc cam or projector to display the assessment and have students complete it on a sheet of paper – For students with visual challenges, email screenshots to their device, or if WiFi is down, use their device to take photos of the assessment.

Digital Activity	Objective	Fail Pivot Ideas
Digital workflow – LMS, Classroom, Website	Sharing assignments, collecting and assessing student work	– COLLECTING WORK: Give a student your phone or an iPad and have him go around to "digitally collect" the work by taking a photo of each screen. Tip: prop the screens up vertically to reduce screen glare. – DISSEMINATING WORK: Project the assignment on a doc cam or projector.
Digitally connecting with another class / expert	Connecting students with peers or experts to expand perspective and ideas	– Have students write a letter to the person or people they were supposed to connect with. Have them ask questions about what they hoped they'd learn and list information they wish they'd have been able to share. Encourage them to wonder about how the other person / people would have thought differently than they do.
Creating videos / audio / images / blogs	Outlet for student creativity / learning—allowing students to synthesize knowledge / understanding	– Give students big sheets of blank paper to graphically organize their plans for this creation. If it's a movie, have them sketch storyboards for their next scene. If it's an audio podcast, prompt them to script out their narration. If it's a blog, have them write or edit their content or design a graphic to go with it.
Accessing digital content: video, text, sound, images	Supplementing instructional content with authentic / engaging materials	– In this case it's always best to have a hard copy downloaded to your desktop in case the WiFi goes down. If the online resource doesn't allow this, consider having alternate resources at the ready in case of emergency.

Now that you're ready to fail forward, you're ready to launch your edventure. Next up is *Part II. Navigating Your Problems.* In the following chapters, I outline some common problems of practice that teachers have shared and that I myself have experienced. These are potential problems of practice to use for your TIEP. I hope you find the problem you isolated in your Gripe Jam in these pages! For each problem, I offer some potential solutions to consider. Remember: These are just starting points. You can always edit and iterate to make these ideas better fit your unique needs. This will help you use your TIEP to chart a course around these obstacles so as to sail further on toward your personal Innovation Island.

part II

NAVIGATING YOUR PROBLEMS

I learned that courage was not the absence of fear, but the triumph over it.

—Nelson Mandela

N ow that we've prepared for our edventure, it's time to set sail. To set your first course, use this section to look for potential new approaches to your problems of practice. Think of this as a menu of problems to sort through. Hopefully some or many will be on your Gripe Jam list. Perhaps others are ones that you didn't remember but could be added to the list of those that plague you.

Throughout this part of the book, we will address four major areas most teachers encounter challenges: differentiation, assessment, classroom environment, and planning instruction. In each section, common problems of practice will be posed and suggestions for possible solutions will be described. Feel free to explore each section from start to finish or thumb through the pages to find your problem of practice. As you read, take notes in your Teacher Innovation Exploration Plan for your action plan and navigation notes for your edventure.

chapter 6

DIGGING INTO DIFFERENTIATION

D ifferentiation. It's a great concept—individualizing learning experiences to the specific needs of each student. Yet how do you create this myriad of learning experiences for *all* of your students? How do you break through barriers of time, space, and materials to support unique needs? The problems that follow plagued my classroom and many of my peers. Hopefully, the suggested solutions will help you plot a course around these floating obstacles.

PROBLEM: SO MANY ABILITY GROUPS, SO LITTLE TIME

I'm sure I'm not the only teacher who laments that the school day is too short. We barely have enough time to teach everything, much less enrich our students' learning with the arts, give them time to burn off some energy, and work on social skills. All day, we're rushing as if we're late for the bus with "Quick, let's learn before the bell rings!" lessons. Add to this the need to differentiate instruction for groups of students, nay, *individual* students with a wide range of ability levels and needs. How is there time for it all?

FIGURE 6.1 Volume of a Pyramid

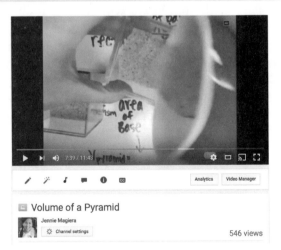

Suggestion: Clone the Teacher

QR Code 6

While the timing of the school day is something that is beyond your control, just try cloning yourself . . . through video lessons (see Figure 6.1)! Scan QR Code 6 to visit the companion website for more resources and examples!

Ingredients for Cloning Yourself

- Computer
- Webcam
- Instructional materials
- Imagination

1. Get your materials together, just as you would teach the actual lesson.

2. Situate yourself in front of your whiteboard or blackboard.

3. Open your webcam.

4. Click "Record."

5. Begin to teach your lesson by recording you writing on a slate, walking students through a math journal page, modeling a science experiment, editing a paper, reading a text, or whatever your students may need!

6. Press "Stop Recording."

7. Upload lesson onto a cloud-based video hosting site or directly onto your students' devices.

8. Repeat steps 1–7 with a video on the same topic, each scaffolded to a different level, as students' needs may dictate.

9. Have students watch videos on based on instructional level, following along on parallel instructional sheets, notebooks. or other materials.

10. Pull students while the class is watching the videos to work one-on-one or in small groups on needed skills.

11. Lather, rinse, and repeat.

QR Code 6

See? Teacher = cloned! This also is possible with a variety of screencasting apps and software currently available for both desktop and mobile devices. Scan QR Code 6 to visit the site and find a list of recommended current screencasting apps and programs available.

Beyond the simple fact that by creating these videos, you are then free to pull small groups to look at slides, dissect a flower, or conduct an experiment, this method offers a myriad of other unique opportunities. For example, the kids can now pause the lesson and rewind if they didn't understand something—a feature that a live lesson with a room full of students would not afford them. Furthermore, absent students who usually miss out on any lessons occurring can now experience the learning virtually from home or once they return. The students now experience a personal, up-close view of all manipulatives and demonstration objects that are being used in the lesson.

While there are video lesson websites available on the web and via mobile apps, there is nothing like your own instruction. It's more personalized for your students as you have a relationship with them, but it's also grounded in the same pedagogy and instructional style your class has grown used to with you. Moreover, you can be sure of its instructional quality. Unfortunately, the same cannot always be said with online video lesson repositories.

By creating these videos, you will be investing in your own future. You will be building a library of differentiated videos to utilize for years to come.

Curating Your Content

As you build your lessons, you will need to consider where you will store and curate them. How will you organize the videos? How will you tag them for later reference? Some things to consider:

Naming Convention

Be thoughtful about how you name the videos. At first, I was naming all of my math videos based on the specific publisher's math curriculum my school used. However, as our school moved away from this program, I realized that "Lesson 2.4" no longer was meaningful to me. Think about naming the videos based on standard or strand. The more consistent your naming convention, the better. If you have the ability to tag the video with common and consistent keywords, even better! For example, "Geometry Lesson" isn't as useful/searchable down the line as "CCSS Math Content 4. G.A.3 Geometry Lesson: Symmetry."

Storage Options

You also want to make a conscious decision about how and where you store the video lessons. Think about storage space, cost, access for students, and whether you hope to share the videos with colleagues. Below are some options:

- **YouTube:** This is an obvious choice as it is widely available, easy to use, easy to share, and has endless storage. You can organize videos into playlists and track content in both the description and title. Additionally, you can make the videos as open or private as you wish with the varied privacy settings. One big problem: Many schools block YouTube for students or even completely.
- **Vimeo:** See above for the flexibility and use. Some added bonuses: It allows for videos requiring a password—an additional privacy option—and some districts that block YouTube leave Vimeo open.
- **Google Drive:** OK, so both Vimeo and YouTube are blocked. You can store videos in Google Drive. However, be cautious about storage limitations based on the type of account you have and the way you upload. You also lose some of the tagging ability in the description. This is also a bit less accessible for others.
- **Hard drive and direct upload:** This is for those who have struggling Internet connections and can't stream multiple videos in a classroom at once. You can directly download the video playlists to student devices before/after school from a main drive and have them loaded and ready to go. While this is the most time-consuming and least convenient, it is also the most secure and least susceptible to Internet issues.

As you create these videos, keep these four important tips in mind:

- **Make it interactive.** Video is a very passive medium. Change it up by posing challenges and tasks for your students to complete as part of the video lesson. Have them complete the same task you're modeling in real-time (i.e., setting up a lab, completing a set of problems, actively reading a passage). Leave Post-It notes, manipulatives, or prompt cards in the middle of the table and give them challenges in the video to complete using these tools. Ask them to pause the video and attack the challenge on their own, then return to the video to reflect on the process.
- **Check for understanding.** Whether it's an exit ticket assessment question they physically turn in, a task they need to complete, or a quick online form, make sure your students are held accountable for the content they view in the video. This prevents them from simply zoning out through all the juicy content you're sharing or opting out of the powerful activities and challenges you're posing.
- **Less is more.** Keep the video to 3–5 minutes or less. As students rewind and pause to complete the video tasks, the time to watch a video with a running time of just a few minutes often multiply threefold or more. Another benefit is that now you can break up lesson content and activities into smaller chunks, allowing for increased differentiation and individualization of video playlists for each student.

- **Embrace imperfection**. The time it should take to make one video should be time it takes to teach the lesson (i.e., 3–5 minutes). If you make a mistake, *keep going*! You're not trying to win an Oscar here. We make mistakes in front of students all the time—doing so in a video, as long as we note it and make it clear to the kids, is just fine. In fact, noting and owning up to mistakes models resilience and iteration to our learners. I used to have my students keep a "Magiera Mistake" tally chart in their notebooks. They loved catching me fail and talking about how I recovered or what I could do better next time. This helped me reflect on my practice and, more importantly, helped my students learn that it's okay to make mistakes.

When I did this in my own classroom, my students often remarked that watching these videos was a highlight of their day. Said one student, "It makes me want to come to school every day 'cause I know that Ms. Magiera got a lesson just for me that day. I don't want to miss my lesson. I like it cause she's—like—talking just to me. It's cool kinda being the only kid in the class."

PROBLEM: KEEPING STUDENTS ENGAGED DURING SMALL-GROUP TIME

Another challenge when it comes to small-group differentiation is that it's hard to know if students are on task when they aren't with you. Are they getting bored and choosing to use this time for something other than the learning task? Are they getting the most out of their learning task? How do they get help when they aren't with you? Here are some approaches to these common quandaries.

Suggestion 1: Choose Your Own Adventure Time

Keeping students on task is easier when they are engaged. There is less impetus to let their minds wander when they are keen on the activity. As such, giving students choice in their task helps with buy-in, motivation, and engagement. Choose Your Own Adventure time achieves this goal.

There are many examples of this. Choice boards give students options while scaffolding their learning. First, create a list of challenges at varying difficulty levels and employing varying learning styles: some hands-on activities, some more cerebral activities, some more auditory activities. It's perfectly fine if they vary in length of completion as well. Then, clearly state the objectives and guidelines for completing the challenge. Finally, consider a way of presenting these directions and challenge topics. One idea is to simply make a board, gridded like bingo card, and allow students to select challenges off of the board. The directions could be index cards affixed to the board, or there may be corresponding directions sheets in another location that match the squares on the board.

Another strategy to do this is digitally. Consider making a website with hyperlinks in each of the gridded boxes. The links would direct students to another page with directions and perhaps even multimedia guidance or catalysts for the challenge. Imagine a student clicks on a box and it takes her to a video challenge where you prompt her to embark on an investigation or create some sort of a project. Or imagine that the box takes a student to an audio file he must decode, translate, or enhance in some way.

Students can be given different levels of achievement for completing the challenges (i.e., finishing five in a row to make a "bingo" or completing a certain number).

Suggestion 2: Self-Differentiating Challenges

If you want to take choice boards to another level, build the assessment into the challenges. As students complete the challenges or assessments, they get immediate feedback and are directed to a set of increasingly difficult tasks or scaffolded supports. This increases the feedback loop and makes more efficient use of small-group learning time. There are several ways to execute this strategy: You can do it with a series of challenge cards or digitally with online forms coupled with a mail merge or through video annotation hyperlinks.

In the case of challenge cards, all you'll need are a set of index cards and perhaps some file folders. Much like a card game, you can set up series of cards with challenges on them. The front poses a challenge or problem, and the back offers multiple-choice answers. For each answer, it directs the student to go to a different card for her next step. Based on the answer, the student will have either a remediation activity, extra practice activity, or challenge activity.

You can store these cards with binder rings or in plastic index card organizers. Consider creating turn-in folders that correspond with each challenge card and placing them in bins with the cards themselves. On the challenge card, instruct students to turn in their work products for each card to its companion folder. This way students presort their own answers into piles of correct, miscue 1, miscue 2, and so on, thereby expediting your grading process. See Figure 6.2 for an example and visit Appendix A and the companion website for a Challenge Card template that you may use in your own classroom.

You can automate this same process digitally with online forms and a mail merge. For example, you could create these same challenges on a Google Form, then use a mail merge add-on such as FormMule to send automated e-mails based on student answers. The mail merge allows you to set each multiple-choice answer to trigger a unique e-mail. Once the students submit

FIGURE 6.2 Challenge Cards

CHALLENGE:

There are eighteen boys and twenty girls going on a field trip. Mrs. Magiera has five parents coming to help chaperone. She will also have her own group. She has to hire a bus to drive them all. Each passenger seat can fit two adults or three students. Each bus has twenty passenger seats. How many busses will Mrs. Magiera need to hire?

Card A: Front

If you think the answer is:

1 bus – go to card B
2 busses – go to card C
3 busses – go to card D

Card A: Back

Card B

Describe how you got this answer on a sheet of paper. Be sure to show all of your work. When you're finished, put your paper in the CARD B folder.

THEN, check out the video here:

Card B: Front

Finished early?

Try the challenges at www.challengemath.com

Card B: Back

Card C

Describe how you got this answer on a sheet of paper. Be sure to show all of your work. When you're finished, put your paper in the CARD C folder.

THEN, write your own word problem that would require similar strategies to solve it!

Card C: Front

Finished early?

Try the challenges at www.challengemath.com

Card C: Back

Card D

Describe how you got this answer on a sheet of paper. Be sure to show all of your work. When you're finished, put your paper in the CARD D folder.

THEN, check out the video here:

Card D: Front

Finished early?

Try the challenges at www.challengemath.com

Card D: Back

QR Code 6

their answer to the challenge, they automatically receive this message with instructions for a differentiated task based on their answer. Visit the companion website (see QR Code 6) for a video walkthrough on how to build this system using Google Forms and the FormMule add-on.

FIGURE 6.3 YouTube Annotation

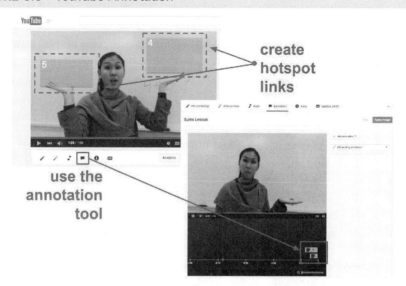

Another option is to build the assessment and differentiation into the same platform. Once you've successfully cloned the teacher, you can make these videos even *more* interactive by including the assessment directly into the video itself. You can do this easily with YouTube video annotation.

YouTube video annotation (see Figure 6.3) allows you to create hotspots within videos that link to other video content on the site. For example, imagine I had created a video lesson about main idea and details. In the video, I situated myself so I was teaching in front of a dry erase board. During the lesson, I displayed the text from a story on the screen and read it aloud to the students. Then I cut to the video of myself in front of the whiteboard and prompted the students to think about the main idea of the story. I then write four options on the board behind me.

Then, using YouTube video annotation tool, I can add hotspot links on the screen so that students viewing the video can click on the answers I had written on the board. When they click on a given answer, it takes them to another video. I can then create four differentiated videos based on the answer choices:

- One video congratulated the students on their thinking for getting the correct answer and then challenged them with a more difficult story or query.
- The other three videos explained why the answer they selected was incorrect and gave them tips on how to avoid the mistake in the future.

Visit the companion website (see QR Code 6) for a video walkthrough on how to build this system using YouTube.

QR Code 6

Assessment Note: As your students complete these challenges, they will want recognition. Badges are a creative and effective option to serve this purpose. As students complete challenges from their challenge cards, YouTube videos, websites, or choice boards, they can gain achievement badges. For more information on badging, see Chapter 7 of this book.

Suggestion 3: Critical Friends

Another way to keep students engaged is to up the accountability ante by assigning them Critical Friends. These pairings match students with like ability to support and encourage one another. Have them write journal reflections on their activities on blogs or in a physical journal. Then give them time to read and respond to their Critical Friend's blog. The benefit of doing this with a digital platform, such as a blog, is that you can have additional readers and supporters to comment on their reflections. Parents, students in other classrooms, colleagues, and even experts in the same field of learning can all boost student confidence by giving helpful tips and feedback. Check out the Twitter hashtag #comments4kids to request comments for your students' blogs and try out one of the many blog sites featured on the companion website.

PROBLEM: FINDING DEVELOPMENTALLY APPROPRIATE DIFFERENTIATED CONTENT

When differentiating for your students, it's one thing to be able to vary the delivery method and student work product but another to find on-level content for your students. Oftentimes, below-grade-level materials are too immature for your students and above-grade-level materials are too thematically complex. So what's a busy teacher with limited resources to do?

Suggestion 1: Create Your Own Content

Instead of waiting for the big-box publishers to catch up to this need or spending large sums of money to purchase the resources that are available, consider some differentiation DIY. As we learned in the previous section, screencasting allows you to build your own lesson content. However, there are additional tools at your disposal as well.

Once you've created a variety of screencast mini-lessons, consider stitching them together into a sequence using tools such as online video playlists. You can create packages of differentiated content based on units of study, student ability level, or various assessments you give each year. These video lesson playlists can be accessible for your students in school but also at home as well.

You can also build your own books using tools such as iBooks Author for Mac and Book Creator for iOS and Android. Visit the companion website (see QR Code 6) for a list of various book creation tools and more ideas for use.

QR Code 6

Suggestion 2: Digital Resources

There is also a myriad of free or low-cost online resources offering scaffolded materials. When looking for differentiated materials, be sure to keep two things in mind: how it is differentiated and the student user interface.

When many publishers differentiate their materials, they simply make texts longer or shorter or provide more or fewer problems. However, the text complexity or structure of the problem remains static. While the length of content does affect its difficulty, many teachers are looking for something a bit more thoughtful when finding differentiated content for their learners. So be sure to examine resources from various levels and see if you agree with their leveling.

QR Code 6

Next, user interface: I find that while the content of some digital resources are terrific, the way in which students must access or interact with the content is too complicated. Look at how intuitive the structure of the program is or is not. Click through various scenarios such as finding the content, interacting with the content, troubleshooting issues, accessing help, or turning in work. The companion website (see QR Code 6) offers some programs I've seen be successful in our schools.

PROBLEM: HOW DO I DISSEMINATE MATERIALS TO STUDENTS AND COLLECT THEIR WORK? (AKA DIGITAL WORKFLOW)

When students are learning in differentiated groups, it becomes difficult to manage the workflow (i.e., disseminating materials and collecting student work). I remember spending hours after school making photocopies, collating small-group packets, color-coding folders, and creating a series of turn-in trays. In the digital classroom, these systems become a bit simpler. Here are some ideas to manage your digital workflow.

Suggestion 1: Learning Management System

A learning management system (LMS) is a digital ecosystem built to support digital workflow. Universities have been using these platforms for years—programs such as Blackboard and D2L. However, they are becoming more and more prevalent in the K–12 learning space—and for good reason.

LMSs such as Edmodo and Schoology have reimagined the user interface to mimic popular social media platforms such as Facebook and Twitter to attract student use. They offer the same helpful tools higher-education LMSs provide, such as assignment creation, digital assignment submission boxes, and electronic quizzes.

However, Edmodo and Schoology also take into account K–12 developmental and programmatic needs. They are effectively device agnostic, meaning that they work on tablets, laptops, and desktops regardless of operating system. Both systems allow students to submit work digitally via app-to-app communication or photo submission. They provide rubric creation tools, badging systems, and point-based grading to allow for quick and easy teacher feedback. For more information on badging, see Chapter 7.

Suggestion 2: Google Classroom

Alternatively, there is Google Classroom—a tool that doesn't quite boast all of the features of a full-fledged LMS but offers full Google integration for you and your students. Google Classroom aims to be the mission control for learning by streamlining the creation and dissemination process for Google docs, sheets, slides, and drawings.

Suggestion 3: Class Websites, QR Codes, and Google Forms

If you're not keen on another student login or third party tool, consider a class website. It's a quick and easy method for sharing class materials, assignments, and information with your students. Another selling point is that it is easier to customize and organize in a way that makes sense to your unique needs and situation.

The challenge with a class website is how does one collect student work? One option is to embed online forms in the site pages, allowing students to submit work virtually. They can send links to their work created on third party programs such as Google Apps or another platform.

Want more help getting started on a website of your own? On the companion website, I share some examples of easy-to-use tools to build your site and tips to get started.

chapter 7

RETHINKING ASSESSMENT

I n the last chapter, we explored possible barriers and solutions to increased instructional individualization (try and say that five times fast). To build on these strategies, we need to better understand our students' strengths and needs. Effective assessment is key to creating personalized learning experiences. In this chapter, we'll dive into the waters of assessment and figure out how to navigate the challenges to get relevant real-time information and keep you sailing in the right direction. If this is where your Teacher Innovation Exploration Plan (TIEP) was centered, take a look at these problems to see if you find yours below. If not, perhaps you'll find another focus that will also solve some problems in your life, bringing you closer to finding that land of different and better!

PROBLEM: I HATE GRADING!

As a classroom teacher, I dreaded grading but loved knowing how my students were doing. Each time I gave any type of assessment, I shivered at the thought of sitting down to grade each one. Moreover, in the time that elapsed between when my kiddos took the assessment and getting the results back to them, they may not be in the same metacognitive learning space (i.e., more learning may have taken place, they may have become more confused, etc.). Thankfully, with some support from our techie tools, we can close this assessment–feedback loop and cut down or completely cut out the grading time.

Suggestion 1: Digital Student Response Software

The first tech tool most people look to are student response systems or "clicker systems." These kits come with a remote control–like "clicker" for each student and software to allow the teacher to give multiple-choice questions and collect quick digital responses from students. While there is a fun aspect to using these tools, they are limited in the types of questions you can

TOOL	DEVICES NEEDED	DESCRIPTION	LINK
Plickers	Projector, teacher device, teacher smartphone or tablet	Website that allows you to upload class lists and generate unique codes for each student. These codes are printed out and display A, B, C, and D, each oriented to face a different edge of the paper. As you ask a multiple-choice question, the student orients his paper so the letter corresponding to the answer faces up. The instructor uses the free app to scan the entire room at once, which digests and analyzes the students' individual responses.	http://www .plickers.com
Kahoot	Teacher device, devices for each student or group of students	Site that allows you to create multiple-choice answers in a game-like interface to quiz students for quick formative assessment	http://www .getkahoot.com
Socrative	Teacher device, devices for each student	Site that allows you to create various question types for both informal formative assessments as well as more formal summative assessments	http://www .socrative.com
Quizlet	Teacher device, devices for each student	Another quiz site that employs flashcard interfaces as well as traditional quizzes and study games	http://www.quizlet .com

ask and can be quite expensive. The good news is that there are some cheap or even free tools out there that allow you to emulate this process without buying the pricey hardware.

Suggestion 2: Learning Management System Assessments

Learning management systems (LMSs) support digital workflow, as you may have seen in the differentiation suggestions in Chapter 6. They also offer robust assessment tools as well. Many of them boast assessment tools that offer more choices than student response software. Their features allow you to embed media directly into the question-and-answer portion of the assessment and offer a wide array of question choices: multiple choice, short answer, long answer, fill in the blank, matching, and sorting.

Suggestion 3: Online Forms

If you want a truly do-it-yourself assessment tool, you can also build your own online forms. Google forms is the most often-used platform for this, as it allows for free and easy form creation. Like the LMS assessments, teachers can select from various question types: short answer, paragraph answer, multiple choice, drop down, checkbox, linear scales, and more. All of the answers can be conveniently displayed both visually as charts, graphs, and summaries as well as in an editable spreadsheet. There are various tools that are constantly evolving to allow for increased automated grading of student form responses. Scan QR Code 7 for an updated list and description of these tools:

QR Code 7

PROBLEM: I NEED TO DIFFERENTIATE ASSESSMENTS BASED ON INDIVIDUALIZED EDUCATION PROGRAM ACCOMMODATIONS AND/OR MODIFICATIONS

It seemed like each year I taught, the number of students with Individualized Education Programs (IEPs) in my classroom grew and grew. And as the number of IEPs grew, so did the number of accommodations and modifications I needed to support. This became especially tricky during assessment time. I needed to find a way to meet the needs of my students with IEPs while also meeting the needs of the rest of my class. How was I going to read aloud each assessment, give stop-the-clock breaks, provide scaffolded tools, and circulate to respond to the questions of everyone else? Here is the trick that increased my ability to serve *all* of my students.

Suggestion: Screencast Assessments

In the previous chapter, I shared the possible use of screencast video lessons to support differentiated instruction (see Chapter 6). In this case, you can also use the screencast strategy to provide differentiated assessments. Imagine reading the test aloud in a video recording and even embedding other accommodations into the recording. You could narrate those stop-the-clock breaks, display on-screen scaffolds such as charts and reference materials, and so on. You could record one version of the assessment and then edit in additional accommodations and modifications as needed.

My students loved these assessments so much. Those with IEPs finally felt like they could have some independence when taking tests. They hated sitting at the "teacher table," always being physically separated from their peers and drawing attention to their special needs. Once we began utilizing the screencast assessment strategy, they took on more agency, empowerment, and confidence.

PROBLEM: MY STUDENTS HAVE A HARD TIME SELF-ASSESSING

While providing real-time feedback in the form of quick exit tickets or assessments is helpful to student learning, it's also important for them to learn to self-assess and reflect on their growth. This can be tricky for students who haven't yet developed metacognitive strategies. Here are a few digital strategies to build these mind muscles.

Suggestion 1: Metacognitive Screencasting

The more I created instructional screencasts for my students, the more they wanted to create their own. At first, it began by my allowing them to create short instructional videos as an anchor activity once they successfully completed an assignment. They were able to screencast their understanding of a concept so as to help their peers who were still struggling. These caught fire and soon, many of our classroom instructional videos were created by my students. It was great to have my students take on this work, but more importantly, it was helpful for me to see my students think through their metacognition when demonstrating concepts or learning.

This evolved into a new form of assessment. Instead of these videos being an anchor activity to keep kids productive after finishing an assignment, they became the assignment itself. I would pose problems to my students

QR Code 7

and ask them to solve it using a screencasting tool or app. Scan QR Code 7 for a list of suggested screencasting tools/apps. They would think through the problem and narrate their thinking as they moved through the problem-solving process. They each were assigned peer reviewers who would watch their video each day and give feedback on their thinking.

They would also fill out a digital form to state their final answer. I would look through their answers and watch the screencasts for students whose answers were particularly surprising, either because they usually struggled with a concept and submitted an accurate answer or because they were so off base.

One year, I had a student who was trying to solve a rates problem. I had presented him with a real-life dilemma I'd faced at the grocery store the previous evening: I wanted to buy some shredded cheese for family Taco Night. The generic cheese was its regular everyday low price, but the fancier name brand was featured on sale if you bought it in bulk. I had to figure out the unit price to determine the better deal. I showed my students a video of myself at the grocery store pondering this challenge and asked them to screen-cast solutions for me.

This particular student wasn't exactly a fan of math class. He pushed back against home-work, schoolwork, lessons, staying in his seat, participating in centers and math games, and basically anything I asked him to do. So when he turned in his screencast with form response stating that his answer was something completely in left field, my automatic assumption was that he was blowing off the assignment.

Well, it turns out it wasn't my student who was wrong. It was me.

As I watched the minute-long video, I not only saw that this young man had found a completely unexpected—and accurate—way to solve the problem but also was an incredible

FIGURE 7.1 Eddie Cheese (https://www.youtube.com/watch?v=5dT_Dr_TVPQ)

(Continued)

(Continued)

mathematician. He used algebraic thinking, modeled his problem using real-world examples, drew out visualizations for his thinking, and even explained his thinking clearly with multiple rationale (see Figure 7.1). The only reason his final submitted answer was incorrect was because of a simple error toward the end of his process.

It turned out that this student wasn't a bad math student—he didn't hate math. I wasn't doing a good job of understanding *how* he processed, synthesized, and shared information. By allowing him to screencast his understanding, I was able to understand his thought process in a new way. I learned that in small groups or one-on-one, he didn't feel comfortable sharing and so shied away from exhibiting his full potential. However, behind a screen, he felt confident to be the math ninja he truly was inside.

The best part of this story comes next. After I saw this student's incredible mathematical thinking, I decided to push my luck to try and get him to correct his mistake. At first, I was going to point out the mistake and ask him to do the problem again. At the last minute, I thought better. Instead, I just asked him to watch his own video. Despite initial frustration at my request, he eventually acquiesced and viewed his masterpiece. At first he was grinning ear-to-ear, nodding along to his own brilliant thinking. And then he got to the point where he made the mistake. He took off the headphones and threw them on the floor and put his head down on the table.

I'd blown it.

But then he sat up, sighed, and said, "I should have labeled my numbers. I mixed up the last two. Can I try this again? I can do better." And it was everything I could do not to burst into tears then and there in front of my class. This young man, who had never wanted to do his homework, his classwork—anything—even *once* now wanted to do something again because he knew he could "do better." #EduWin

Suggestion 2: Digital Portfolios

As students continue to create more robust work to show what they know, it's important to give them a platform to curate and reflect upon that work. Student work portfolios aren't anything new. In fact, I have an entire closet containing folders of my grade-school projects that I can't bear to part with. The good news is that as we enter the digital age, more of this work is becoming digital (Yay! More closet space for future generations!). The bad news is that creating student portfolios is no longer as simple as putting weather reports into manila folders.

Not to fear, there are a myriad of options that not only allow you to collect and save student work but also provide new and improved methods for student self-assessment and reflection. These digital portfolio tools allow you to use cameras from your smartphone, tablet, or computer to upload quick images or videos. They also allow you to attach digital content such as links, cloud-based documents, and videos. Many of the sites allow for comments and reflection as well. They range from the quick and easy tools to much more sophisticated platforms. Some current options include the following (Note: You may also visit the companion website to see an updated list of options available.):

TOOL	DESCRIPTION	PROS/CONS	AGE RANGE	WEBSITE
SeeSaw	This is a platform that was designed specifically for creating digital portfolios. It does so well and very simply. SeeSaw allows students to easily upload media and text to a portfolio page. They can receive comments and encouragement from others. At the end of the year, with the paid version, you can export or migrate data.	Pro: Very simple to use—great for young students. Works across platforms on most devices Con: May be too simplistic for older students Cost: Free for 10 classes, with content expiring after year is over. Purchase required for pro features, such as downloading/maintaining content beyond 12 months	All ages	http://web.seesaw.me
Three Ring	Three Ring is another platform designed specifically for digital portfolios. It is similar to SeeSaw, so users would need to check out both sites to see which seems to better fit their needs and style.	Pro: Works across platforms on all devices. Many features available to use Con: For some, the features may be overwhelming Cost: Purchase required	All ages	http://www.threering.com
KidBlog	This blog website allows students to create their own blogs as part of a class. Teachers can moderate student blogs and provide support. Students can publish work they are proud of in blog posts with an accompanying description of why they selected it for their portfolio.	Pro: Allows for easy commenting, sharing with families, and media uploads. Easy to take from class to class and year to year and share across classrooms or even across the school Con: Some older students prefer to have a more sophisticated blog platform, such as WordPress or Blogger. Cost: Purchase required	Primary–middle school	http://www.kidblog.com
Google Drawings	This web-based drawing tool found within Google Drive is actually a great way for students to record their work. See the text box below for ideas on how to use it!	Pro: Flexible in use, allows for student creativity when building their portfolio. Allows students to easily grow and maintain the same portfolio over the years	Intermediate–high school	http://drive.google.com

(Continued)

(Continued)

TOOL	DESCRIPTION	PROS/CONS	AGE RANGE	WEBSITE
		Con: Students must have a Google for Education login to use this tool. Does not work well on tablet devices Cost: Free		
EduClipper	This site is essentially Pinterest for teachers and students! Clip resources from the Web to curate content—a great way to capture ongoing student digital work.	Pros: This is a simple and powerful tool that not only allows your students to create their own digital portfolio but also to curate content from the Web for learning purposes! Cons: Not on Android yet Cost: Free	All ages	http://www.educlipper.net

Some things to note when creating digital portfolios:

- **Curation is key**: Although now there's no longer a limit on what students can keep around, we still want to think about curating student work. Give your students a framework for determining what work makes it into the portfolio, and why. Ask them to attach a reflection on this process to each piece of work, explaining why they are proud of it, what they think they did well, and how they could improve it in the future. Perhaps as the portfolio builds, this reflection could also include a piece about how this work fits in with their overall portfolio. Just as an artist curates his or her collection, so should your students as they make their selections.

- **Encourage commenting**: Students thrive on feedback. Make sure you give frequent feedback on their portfolios, but also invite their families to have ready access. Since these portfolios are no longer physical items that will get battered or lost through trips home and back, parents should be able to see their student's portfolio grow on a daily basis. For the younger students, this will help as their families support their homework and growth. For older students, this can be a support in applying to colleges and in looking for job opportunities in the future.

- **Use them for goal setting**: The digital portfolios, if done well, are an amazing snapshot of student progress. Therefore, take advantage of them when conferencing with your students and/or their families. Use the current and past work to see growth and set new goals. Note this within the digital portfolio or on another document to track how these conversations help shape and improve the portfolio—this will also be good feedback for your own practice.

THE DRAW OF GOOGLE DRAWINGS

Google Drawings, at first glance, is a simple web-based drawing tool found in Google Drive. However, there are many more features and use cases embedded within it.

- **Revision History:** Remember, one of the benefits of Google Drive is that it frequently autosaves your files. Therefore, file types in Google Drive have the ability to look back at the file revision history—the various previous autosaved versions of the file. If you click on "File" in a Google Doc, Sheet, Slide, or Drawing, you will see the option "Revision History" (see Figure 7.2). This is helpful when you're writing a paper and you accidentally delete something or you're collaborating on a slide deck and a colleague changes some of your work. This feature is especially useful in Google Drawings. In this file type, the changes are much more visual. You can use the arrow keys within the Revision History window to see the changes happening—the drawing seems to move like a GIF (moving image). This is great to look back at student metacognition—why did they sort that shape into that category? Why did they rearrange that idea in the graphic organizer? It's also great to see the progress or growth on a single assignment or digital portfolio.

FIGURE 7.2 Digital Portfolio—Revision History

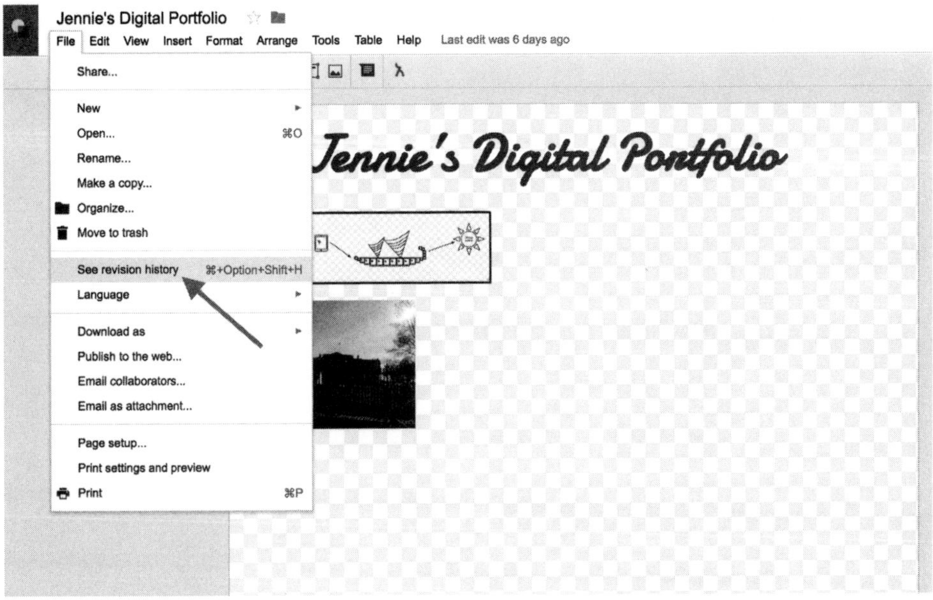

- **Commenting and Hyperlinking Objects:** In a Google Drawing, you can insert a myriad of shapes: lines, circles, polygons, speech bubbles, prisms, and so on. You can also insert images from your hard drive, device camera, or even through a Google Image Search directly from within the drawing app itself. All of these objects in a Google Drawing—even text boxes—can be commented on (see Figure 7.3). If you click on the object and then click the comment icon in the toolbar (a small gray rectangular speech bubble), you can add a comment directly connected to the object. This is terrific for giving feedback or for having students add captions or notes to their drawing. You can also hyperlink objects to another webpage or Google Drive file, turning them into buttons (see Figure 7.4).

FIGURE 7.3 Digital Portfolio—Commenting

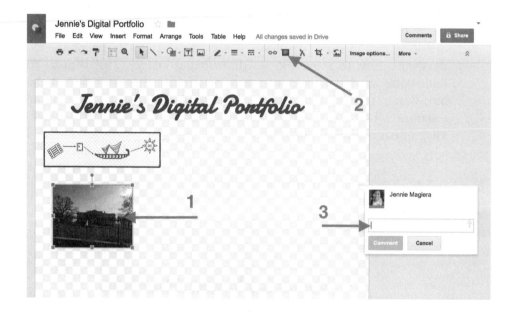

FIGURE 7.4 Digital Portfolio—Hyperlink

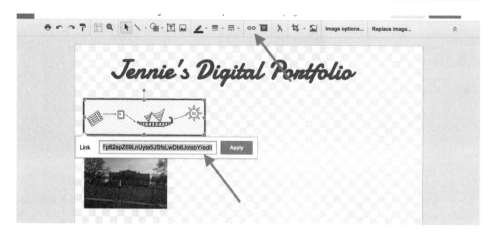

For example, you could insert an image or shape of a star, then click on it and hyperlink that object to a Google Doc report on constellations or a YouTube video about the stars.

- **Expandable Canvas**: The canvas, or drawing area, on Google Drawings is easily expandable (see Figure 7.5). Simply pull out from the bottom right corner of the canvas and voilà—more working space! If you've run out of space to expand, click on the "View" menu on the toolbar and then select "50%" to zoom out. Then you have more space to expand the canvas.

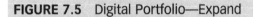

FIGURE 7.5 Digital Portfolio—Expand

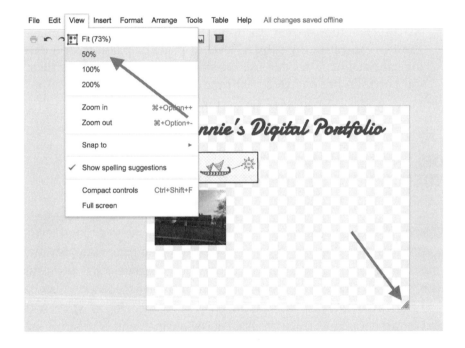

- **Embedding in Google Sites**: Google Drawings can easily be embedded into a Google Site. As you edit your site, select the "Insert" menu. Then look for the Google Drive icon. Under this menu, you will find Google Drawings as an option. Once you've found your Drawing file and inserted it, you're done! As the drawing is updated from the Drawing file itself, it will automagically update on the website as well!

With these four features, you can easily have students create dynamic digital portfolios. Here's a step-by-step guide on how to do this:

QR Code 7

1. Create a Google Site. Title it with your class name. *(Never used Google Sites before? No worries—scan QR Code 7 to check out the companion website for a quick tutorial.)*

2. Create a page on the site for each of your students.

QR Code 7

3. Create a blank Google Drawing for each of your students. *(Note: You can use Google Classroom for this. If you've never used Google Classroom before, visit the companion website or scan QR Code 7 for a tutorial.)*

4. Embed the student's Google Drawing in their page on your site.

5. Ask students to do the following:

   a. Add photos or screenshots of their curated work.

   b. If the work is digital, click on those images and add a link to the work.

   c. Add a comment onto the image to add a reflection for why they selected that work.

6. As students add to their portfolio, they can rearrange the images to show organization by subject, level of pride or passion, or a chronological timeline. They can use revision history to show how their digital portfolio has changed over time.

7. Don't forget to share this site with families!

PROBLEM: TEACHING STUDENTS HOW TO GIVE PEER FEEDBACK

If you want to take student reflection and self-assessment to another level, pair them up with a Critical Friend to get peer feedback (see Figure 7.6). For me, this was a challenge. I had to find a way to cultivate the reflective and trusting student mindset, language, and culture needed for effective peer feedback. I also had to build structures and systems for regular sharing and responding to work—one that allowed for absent partners, like or unlike ability pairings, and both struggling and excelling students to get quality feedback.

Suggestion 1: Google Drive

Google Drive facilitates sharing and collaboration so it is an easy choice for facilitating peer feedback. Students can create shared folders in which they place work and their Critical Friend can respond. Google Drive files have helpful built-in tools for feedback. Google Docs allow for students to enter one of three modes: Editing, Suggesting, and Viewing (see Figure 7.7). Suggesting functions much like Track Changes in Microsoft Word, but with a completely different view, so the document owner can see a version both with and without the suggested edits. All Google Drive files (Docs, Sheets, Slides, and Drawings) allow for element-based commenting. That is, critical friends can select a section of text, image, or object and attach a comment.

FIGURE 7.6 Critical Friend

Critical Friend Feedback

Title of student work

Your answer

Link to student work

Your answer

Critical Friend - author

Your answer

Critical Friend - reviewer

Your answer

Effort

	1	2	3	4	5	
Author didn't seem to show pride in work	○	○	○	○	○	It was clear author gave full effort and showed pride in work

Glows

Your answer

Grows

Your answer

SUBMIT

FIGURE 7.7 Editing, Suggesting, and Viewing

Suggestion 2: Google Drive and Google Forms

While it's helpful for students to get feedback directly in their work, it's difficult to track feedback over time. This method also poses a challenge for the teacher. To track whether Critical Friends are giving feedback and to coach them on the quality of that feedback, the teacher has to open multiple documents and search for embedded comments and suggestions. One alternate idea is to pair Google Drive folder sharing with a Google Form. Students review their Critical Friend's work and fill out a Google Form with their overall feedback and a link to the work. The corresponding Google Form will act as a record of feedback and progress over time. Additionally, it means the teacher only has to check one place to observe the feedback process between the Critical Friends.

Suggestion 3: Blogging and Quadblogging

Just as Kidblog is a powerful digital portfolio tool, it's also a terrific system for feedback. As students curate their work, they can gather reactions and support from their Critical Friends or an authentic audience by way of blog commenting.

Want to extend your students' Critical Friends and audience beyond the walls of your classroom? Quadblogging.com allows you to match up with three other classrooms that match your desired affinity groups (location, age, etc.). Each week, a different class is the focus group and receives feedback from the other three in their quad. You and the other teachers can take it a step further by assigning Critical Quads or four students across the four classes who always respond to each other's work. This way, you are building relationships among these students and allowing them to get consistent feedback.

If you decide to quadblog, consider what topics you'd like to have your classes discuss and how communicating beyond the walls of your classroom will support your students. Consider creating norms for giving feedback as discussed above. In fact, this may be a good thing to try after first practicing how to give effective feedback within your class through Google Drive and Forms. Once your students are ready, head to the site to connect your classes—and off you go!

ACCOUNTABILITY WITHOUT ASSESSMENT: GAMIFICATION AND ACHIEVEMENT BADGES

Assessment. It's a hotly debated topic—big tests, small tests, short answer, long answer, no tests, more projects. At the end of the day, we need to keep in mind *why* we assess at all:

- To learn more about what our students know and can do
- To keep our students accountable for learning goals
- To keep our students motivated to achieve

As you continue on your edventure, take a pit stop with me to explore an alternative to traditional assessment—one that may solve many of your problems not only of grading but also student motivation and even differentiation. Let's talk about badging and gamification.

Many of us earned badges in our childhood scouting troops. Today, in addition to earning badges in these groups, students earn both badges and points in the apps and video games they play. As such, many schools have begun taking advantage of this idea to both acknowledge student achievement and encourage students to set higher goals and try more difficult challenges. This is one aspect of what is referred to as *gamification*—the use of game mechanics in the design of a nongame context, such as the classroom. In Chapter 6, I mentioned badges as an option for keeping students motivated and accountable for free choice time. Gamification and badges can be used throughout your teaching to support students in assessing their work as well as their social skills.

The concept of badging is pretty simple. Students complete tasks or challenges and earn a recognition badge. Just as you got "Fab Fishing" badge for catching that carp in scouts, you can earn a "Fillin' It Up" badge for correctly using volume formulas to find the capacity of classroom objects. Badges can be one-time achievements or can be leveled up. For example, that "Fillin' It Up" badge can have a Level 1–3, where you add stars to the badge for finding the capacity of more and more complex objects.

While badging systems can range from the very simple to full-on game-based systems, they tend to have a few things in common:

- Naming: Badges are simply named and have some sort of a visual icon attached (see Figure 7.8 below for examples).
- Nonlinear progression: Badges can be leveled—meaning you must achieve Level 1 badges before attempting Level 2 badges—but there is no clear single starting point. It should not be a linear path. Instead, it's more a choose-your-own-adventure concept. Students can peruse the various challenges and start with the one that speaks to their interests, strengths, or goals.
- Evidence based: Badges have clearly stated criterion and evidence required for being earned. If the method to achieve the badge is too vague, it will lead to confusion, the student doing something other than you had hoped, or both. So for the "Fillin' It Up" badge, I might state: "Students must find an object in the classroom marked with an orange X and use their powers of mathematics to solve for the capacity of the object without anything but a ruler, a sheet of paper, and a

pencil. Once the student has completed this task, submit the paper to the teacher for badge recognition."

- **Submission system**: Badge systems have a clear method for submitting evidence and receiving recognition. Be it a screenshot, narrative essay, or file upload, they should know what evidence to collect to prove they have earned the achievement. Note that most digital badging systems have features to accept evidence (more on system options below). In older grades (usually Grades 3 and up), I like to assign evidence checking to a team of students who review the evidence on a weekly basis. Then we have ceremonies once a week to award badges to those who've earned them. Again, this makes the badging seem more egalitarian and gives students more ownership of the process.

Once you have started to build your badging system, you want to make sure it will work. The trick to a successful badging system is get everyone to buy in, which simply put is to make your students *care* about it. When cultivating

FIGURE 7.8 Sample Badge Menu

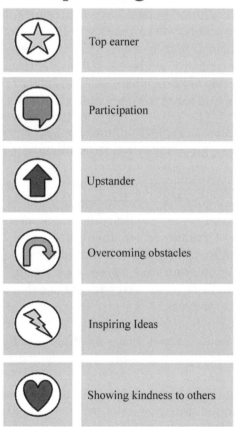

Sample Badge Menu

Top earner

Participation

Upstander

Overcoming obstacles

Inspiring Ideas

Showing kindness to others

that care, there are two types of motivation to keep in mind: prize motivation and social motivation.

Prize motivation is the usual go-to with badging. Think of frequent flyer programs or even those "buy 10 subs get one free" cards. Those all convince to you take certain actions you may not have normally—purchase that slightly more expensive flight, drive another two minutes out of your way to get *that* sub—because you want the prize associated at the end. You want access to upgraded seats or to earn that free sub. If done well, the individuals involved don't even really consider if the prize is worth the effort—the prize itself is the focus. However, the prizes in our classroom are a bit more limited and perhaps a bit less enticing: grades, stickers, food. There are certainly some good examples: I've even seen instances where more badges lead to more freedom or privileges in the school. Nonetheless, this is type of motivation is fleeting. Remove the prize—or interest in the prize—and remove the incentive to carry out the action. So while prize motivation may be a good start to build care toward a badging system, it alone cannot and should not stand alone.

Social motivation is the stronger of the two. This is when the individual is engaging in actions not for the sake of the prize but because they buy in to the system itself due to a social aspect. For example, I frequently use a social app called Swarm by FourSquare. This app allows you to check into locations to record your travels, restaurants, and favorite locations but also to show your friends where you are. To encourage you to check in, you get badges for different achievements. I recently got a badge for checking into a coffee shop five times! Woo hoo! What did I win? Nothing! But I got a little message that told me I had dethroned one of my friends as the "mayor" of that particular coffee shop, meaning I'd been there more than he had. What did I get for being the mayor? Nothing! And yet I was near-delirious with glee at beating him. Yes, I did go to that particular coffee shop that day because I knew I needed *one more check in* to beat him. My friend was quite upset and spent the next week over-caffeinating himself to win back his crown (as of the time I'm writing this, he has yet to do so).

OK, so in the example of Swarm, social motivation has us drinking and spending too much money on overpriced caffeine. But what if we could use this power for good, to get our students to tackle classroom problems with that much zeal? The question is this: How do you build social motivation? To do this, the teacher must first care about it. Make it a big deal in class, create an exciting and public display for it in your classroom, hype it up daily with students, and refer to it often. In games, points are always visible. You can see the leaderboard and it motivates to you push higher. If your students see you care about it, they'll have more buy-in.

Additionally, be sure to publicly celebrate achievements. When someone is pulling ahead, rather than quietly handing out a badge, make an announcement through your board or out loud. If you're using a digital announcement system through a LMS or website, post it there on the front page. Just as Swarm announced to both my friend and me that I was the new mayor of the coffee shop, so must you acknowledge movements within your system.

Once you begin to build this system, make sure a good percentage of the badges are easily achievable. Think of those games so many of us play—candy smashing, league building, bird tossing games. The first few levels are pretty simple. You quickly rack up points and achievements and think, "Hey, I'm pretty good at this." Then all of the sudden you hit that one challenge and get stuck. If it happens too soon in the game you may get frustrated, give up, and think, "Well, that game wasn't for me." If it happens *after* you've experienced enough success to feel like you're winning overall—this is just one setback—you may be more inclined to persevere and try again. You may even invest more into winning—asking for help from a friend, looking up codes online, buying extra lives. This is the kind of perseverance and resourcefulness we hope to see in our students when they are attacking a problem in our classrooms. So as you create your badging system, test it out yourself—are there enough easy badges to win? Are they differentiated so that students of varying ability, strengths, and needs can access a good number of them right away? If not, shift toward more on the easy end. The good news is that if your kids exceed your expectations, you can always add new levels and new badges. In the world of education, there is no final stage, no final boss. There's always more to learn.

Other tips: While many badging systems are digital, I encourage my colleagues to scaffold into the virtual platforms by creating physical badges for their students to proudly display on lockers, desks, or on a wall.

There are a variety of tools to help you manage badging. The simplest is to use a site created just for this such as Class Badges, Credly, or Open Badges. These websites allow you to create, issue, and manage student virtual badges. However, if you're already using a LMS or are planning on trying one out, check to see if they have a built-in badging tool as many do, such as Schoology and Edmodo.

While it's important for the badges to be specific, it's also fun to create a few with a bit of whimsy. This allows for students who have a difficult time achieving academically to dig into the concept and have a bit of fun. Include these bonus badges as well as others with more serious goals, all at varied levels of difficulty.

Moreover, badging can be used to encourage positive behaviors as well. I like having my students also create badge suggestions during class congress meetings, giving them a sense of agency in the system. Take a look at Figure 7.8 for some examples of badging criteria and types.

Badging is one aspect of gamifying your classroom. You can use this as part of small-group learning or as a foundation to your entire class ecosystem. If you're interested in learning more about badging and gamification, I suggest the following resources:

- Website Tool

  - Rezzly—A gamified content creation platform for students and teachers (http://www.rezzly.com)

- Book

  - *Reality Is Broken: Why Games Make Us Better and How They Can Change the World* (2011) by Jane McGonigal

- TED Talks

  - "Gaming Can Make a Better World" by Jane McGonigal (http://bit.ly/janeted)
  - "The Game Layer on Top of the World" by Seth Priebatsch (http://bit.ly/sethtedtalk)

chapter 8

CREATING A POSITIVE
CLASSROOM ENVIRONMENT

Students learn better when they are in a positive environment. It may seem a simple and obvious statement, but creating that positive environment isn't always quite so easy. Different situations, communities, school cultures, and external elements all factor into the climate of a classroom. In this chapter, we'll illuminate various challenges that arise when trying to develop this positive culture and explore some ideas for how to overcome them. Even if your Teacher Innovation Exploration Plan (TIEP) is already started, perhaps one of the new ideas in this chapter will convince you to change course—or perhaps you came straight here to find your struggle. If you haven't noticed already, many of these problems relate to one another— for example, a positive classroom environment can help facilitate better student collaboration and peer assessment. Remember that the suggestions in this chapter are just that—suggestions. Feel free to take pieces of ideas shared throughout these pages and remix them to create your own action plan for your TIEP!

PROBLEM: CREATING A CULTURE OF RESPECT AND COLLABORATION

Sometimes it's difficult to get to the meat and potatoes of teaching and learning because the culture isn't quite there yet. Whether it be student relationships with one another, a chatty classroom, or individual students struggling with the class environment, sometimes the biggest challenge is helping everyone get along and get on board. There are many books and resources out there that outline strategies for building a positive classroom environment. However, here are a few of my favorite digital strategies to get you going.

Suggestion 1: Mood Check-Ins

Sometimes when students come to school upset, it's about something that happened at home or on their way to school, or it may be a more prolonged personal issue. Sometimes they don't feel fully comfortable voicing these problems aloud or perhaps don't find the time to talk to an adult in the busy cadence of the school day. Mood check-ins provide a structure for our students to share their needs and feelings. At first, this was a quick clothespin by the door whereby the students would indicate their mood. This didn't quite work as it was too visible (and thereby it didn't feel fully safe) and didn't provide a mechanism for kids to share more details or request specific support. Then I tried half-sheet paper forms—this worked better, as it felt more private to the students and they would write more details, but it was cumbersome to facilitate and difficult to track over time.

FIGURE 8.1 Mood Check-In

And then there was Google Forms. As you may have read from other chapters, Google Forms is not only a free and simple way to create an online form, but it also aggregates all responses into an easy-to-read spreadsheet. Students came in every day and filled out their Google Form mood check-in, checking off their various feelings, explaining their mood, setting a goal for class, and indicating if they needed a conference with me (see Figure 8.1). I was able to use conditional formatting to quickly draw attention to certain flagged moods or keywords and whether the students requested a conference.

By checking in on their emotional state first thing, I was able to put out fires before they got out of hand (i.e., student-to-student conflict, a child feeling ill, someone who is dealing with a troubling issue at home, bullying, etc.). There were many instances when we discovered ongoing serious wellness issues that were going unaddressed due to the absence of a structure for safe and private reporting. Students internalized the understanding that teachers want to know how they are and are safe to speak to. This strategy encourages kids to write in about all sorts of issues, both happy and sad, making student–teacher relationships with each of them stronger and more positive (see Figure 8.2).

FIGURE 8.2 Mood Check-In Responses

	How do you feel today?	Why do you feel this way?	Create one goal for today	Teacher Conference?
	nervous, scared	Because my cousin got jumped by a group of boys.	word and use it in a very great sentence.	No
	tired, sleepy	I feel this way because I didn't get no sleep	one goal for my day is to stay on eagle	No
	happy, thrilled, excited, energized, proud, beaming	I have not been late or absence since the first day of school and that makes me feel good.	my goal for today is to get on eagle and stay on eagle	No
	tired, sleepy, nervous, scared, irate, angry	I wasup all night then had to walk to school. I'm hungry now.	togethappy	Yes
	happy, thrilled, chill, relaxed, calm	I'm going too get my homework done	Too do all my homework	Yes
	happy, thrilled	I had fun this weekend	be nice	No

Suggestion 2: Class Dojo for Encouraging Positive Action

Class Dojo is a robust yet simple tool for class management (see Figures 8.3 and 8.4). It allows you to create classrooms populated with virtual student avatars (which the students can customize). Then you can determine various positive behaviors to be encouraged and negative behaviors to be discouraged. As these behaviors are exhibited, the teacher can reinforce positive behaviors by awarding Dojo Points. The result is real-time feedback for the student. Students can set point goals each day and use this platform to take ownership of their actions. This is somewhat related to the concept of badges or gamification that was mentioned in the previous chapter.

FIGURE 8.3 Class Dojo 3

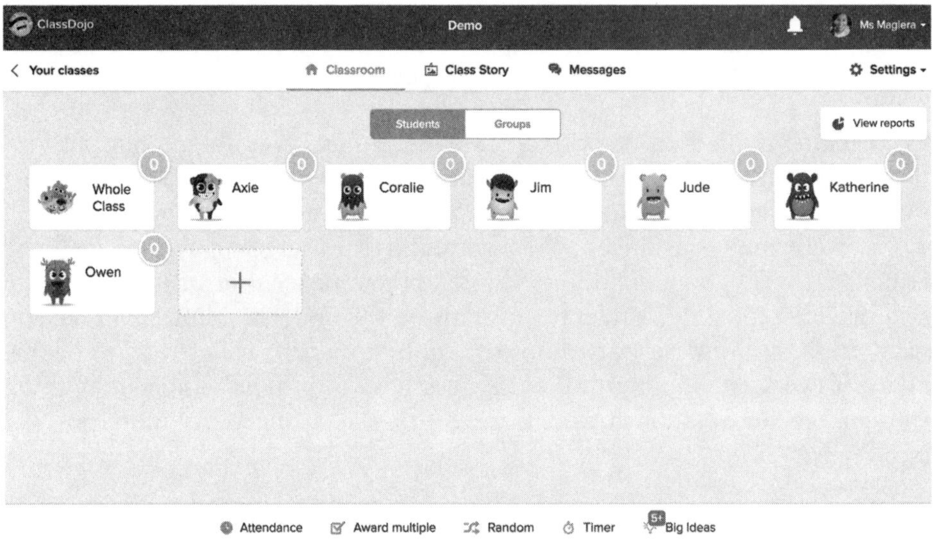

FIGURE 8.4   Class Dojo 4

Suggestion 3: Using Music to Set the Mood

Sometimes students are chatting to fill the silence. Using music to set the mood and fill the room picks up energy in the morning, calms kids down post-lunch, and helps my anxious students find a beat to their work. Transitions, work time, tests, small groups—they all can have their own playlist. Hook your computer up to a set of speakers, find the right playlist and voilà! You can magically change the mood and instruction using music.

This is a fun and low-stress method to cue students to different tasks, moods, and periods of the day. It can replace some of the more militant procedures in a classroom (clapping to get students' attention, transitioning in lines with arms folded, silent transitions). It is amazing to see a student trudge in from the snow after a bad morning and then—Bam!—they are shaking their hips to Shakira and greeting classmates with a grin. Come time for the math challenge, my normally frustrated students would start tapping their feet, putting pencil to paper when I played the math message playlist. Off-task chatting all but ceased during work time as students would quiet down to listen to the instrumental work-time playlist, piping up only to share an idea with a peer or collaborate with a group.

Some examples of tunes and times:

> *Morning Playlist:* I love to use popular, upbeat songs with a positive message. As kids enter the classroom, they dance in listening to "Waka Waka (This Time for Africa)" by Shakira, "Firework" by Katy Perry, and "Wavin' Flag" by K'naan. There are also playlists curated in popular Internet radio sites that feature positive playlists.

Thinking Cap Playlist: This is the time for our kids to problem solve and challenge themselves with difficult problems. Therefore, this playlist is more mellow but still has a "you can do it" message. They work listening to either "The World's Greatest" by R. Kelly or "Wake Up Everybody" by John Legend.

Working and Smiling Playlist: When it is time for kids to work but lyrics would be distracting, I turn to Vitamin String Quartet. A fellow teacher told me about this group—as the name suggests, they are a string quartet who performs popular music (Queen! Michael Jackson! Lady Gaga!). It's pretty funny the first time you hear it, but a fitting background soundtrack for worktime!

Transition Playlist: We do an action-movie slo-mo transition. Kids know where to go and begin transitioning as soon as the music turns on. They make ridiculous slo-mo faces and overexaggerated movements and have a total ball moving from their seats to centers, the bathroom line, and so on. In this way, 25 kids can get from Point A to Point B safely without pushing and while still smiling. The perfect song for this is from the Kill Bill soundtrack: "Battle Without Honor or Humanity" by Tomoyasu Hotei. For added fun, consider awarding an "Oscar Winner" for best silent and slo-mo transition.

Here is some feedback from my students on this strategy:

HOW DOES THE MUSIC IN OUR CLASSROOM MAKE YOU FEEL?

The music makes me feel good because we use it for when we are doing our work and it makes me feel calm inside.

The music makes me feel calm and it cheers me up when I'm mad or I got in trouble. When I listen to the music, I don't have to be mad.

I like listening to music in class because when I am not in a good mood, the music makes me feel happy again.

It makes me happy and it makes me focus better, sometimes it is a way that everyone connects in the class (with music).

The music makes me feel calm. I like the beats, like sometimes when she plays Katy Perry ("Firework") and I would dance and sing to the tune.

It makes me feel happy during transition 'cause we make it more fun than just walking and sometimes it stops me from talking a lot.

I love the music; it makes me feel thrilled and happy. I like when we have music when we work and in the morning and during the transition. It helps me concentrate and helps me by telling me when to stop or when to go. It is really helpful and some of the songs I hear I be singing along.

I love the music because it helps me relax. I like the morning music because it is the main music; you know, it gets you energized. I also like the work time music; I love to hear the violins in my ear.

We have music in the morning, during transitions, in the math message, and in work time. It makes me feel relaxed and it makes me concentrate with my work.

The songs make me feel happy in the morning and in the evening; they make me feel relaxed and good; and in the transition, it makes me feel happy/funny inside. That is how the music and transition makes me feel.

The music makes me feel like it is a good morning.

The music makes me feel so energetic because when you are going slow eating, then the music comes on and it makes us go fast. The time we do music is during math message, in the morning, and also sometimes during transitions. Emotions for the music: happy, peaceful, calm

I like the music in the morning, the transition, and the music in work time because it makes me feel happy. Like in the work time, the music makes me stay on task. And in the morning, I can enjoy myself all the time while eating (that is one of my favorite things to do).

Music makes me feel excited during morning entry because it helps me think better and clears my head. I like the beat and the words. It helps me calm down when I'm upset. I also like the slow-motion transition because it's fun and I get to express myself.

We hear the music during math message and it help me concentrate more.

I like to listen to music in the morning because it is calming and helps you to get energy. Also because it is fun makes your day go smooooooth and not bumpy. The music can also teach you about people and make you feel better, like the song goes "You may think that I'm a 0. But hey I'm a superstar just be who you are."

I really enjoy listening to music because it makes me feel calm. We listen to music at transition and when we come in the morning. I hope get to listen to music next year in my classroom.

PROBLEM: SUPPORTING STRUGGLING STUDENTS

As all educators know, some students require more support than others when it comes to self-monitoring and making good choices. Many times, we address this need through behavior contracts and various goal-setting tools. Here are two ideas to reimagine these strategies.

Suggestion 1: Blogging

As mentioned above, blogging allows students to self-reflect and share their learning. However, it is also a method to help students keep track of their own positive behaviors. Consider having your students set goals for each day, subject, or activity. Then give them a few minutes at the end of each period to reflect on their effort, productivity, and achievements through blogging. They can share how they did in progressing toward their goal and add in videos, images, and student work to enhance their reflection. Invite their support network (family, school staff, friends, etc.) to view and comment on their blog posts. You can make this support as private or public as the child and family sees fit, depending on the student's needs and anonymity requirements.

Suggestion 2: Positivity Timelines

For students who need more of a concrete structure, consider a positivity timeline (see Figure 8.5). Using tools such as Google Drawings (found in Google Drive), your students can track their work in timed increments.

FIGURE 8.5   Timeline

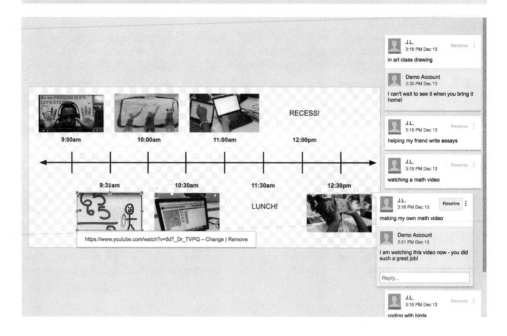

Set a time interval that makes sense based on the student's need. Each time that interval passes (timed with a digital clock on their device or a simple kitchen timer), they take a student work selfie. This could be a literal selfie of themselves doing work or a screenshot of something on they are working on digitally. They then add this image to their timeline and write a five-word description of what they are doing. Share this Google Drawing with their support network and encourage them to leave comments in the Google Drawing to encourage the student. If the student is working on a digital product, she can link the student work selfies to the video, Doc, or other web-based file.

Not only does this allow students to track their positive work habits, but it also creates a digital portfolio of their learning. Families and school staff can collaborate to support the student without fear of losing paper contracts or charts. Moreover, student work and progress is all saved in one handy-dandy location!

PROBLEM: COMMUNICATING WITH FAMILIES

One idea for building positive classroom culture is to involve families. Communicating with parents and guardians about their child can help bridge support from school to home and back again. As it's important that we call home for positive reasons as well as challenges, this communication can get quite time consuming and difficult to keep track of. Here are some ways to streamline parent communication and make sure you're keeping a good balance of super student calls and problem-solving calls.

Suggestion 1: Class Dojo for Communication

While Class Dojo is beneficial for encouraging positive behavior, it can also be used to communicate with parents. Not only can families see their child's Dojo points but the teacher can also send alerts and notifications such as photos of class work, reminders about school events, and so on. Parents can write back to the teacher, and all communication is saved on the platform. Class Dojo is device agnostic (i.e., works on any mobile or desktop platform) so it makes it super accessible for most families (see Figure 8.6).

FIGURE 8.6 Class Dojo Messenger

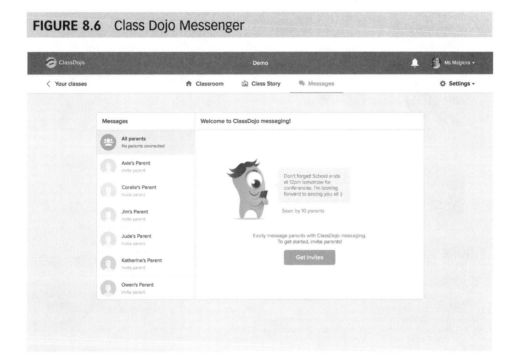

Suggestion 2: Google Forms

Sometimes it helps to have all of your parent communication in one place. This allows you a reference point of who you spoke with and when. Once again, Google Forms is a response to this need. Create a Google Form survey collecting name, e-mail address, phone number, and comment. Post this on a class website or share the link at parent–teacher conferences. As the form is filled out, you will collect data in that handy-dandy self-populating spreadsheet. The result? A quick reference for who you need to call or e-mail back and a centralized place to log follow-up communication. You can also set notification rules to e-mail you every time someone fills out the form so you don't have to keep checking it.

One of the surprise added benefits was that my students quickly realized that they could submit the forms themselves to get in touch with me. As you can see in Figure 8.8 below, many of the submissions were from my class asking for help or sharing issues they were having. This lead to me creating a separate form for student needs (see Figures 8.7 and 8.8).

FIGURE 8.7 Contact Ms. Magiera

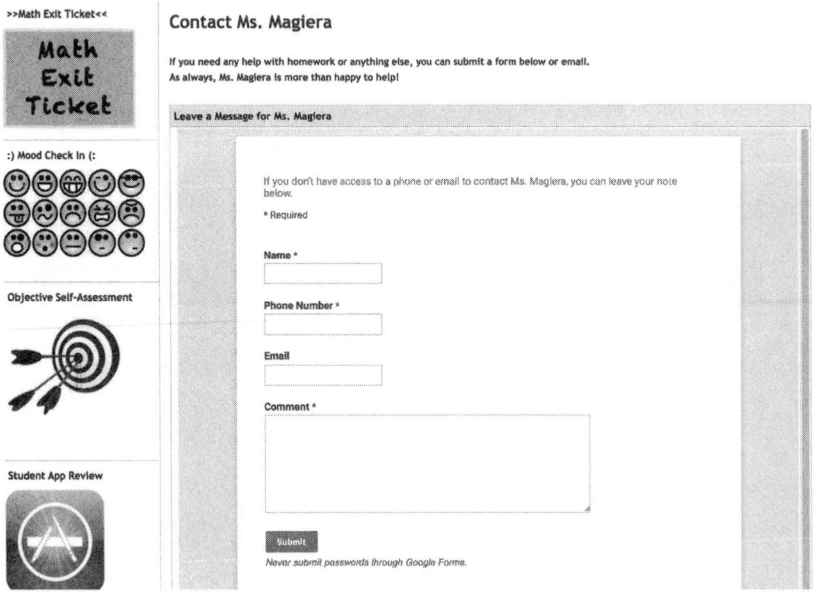

FIGURE 8.8 Contact Me Responses

1	Comment	Responded?	Responses Notes
2	Hi Ms. Magiera, Can you please call me back to discuss [ ]'s homework?	9/2 @ 5:11pm - Call	
3	Heyyyyy Ms.Magiera when do you want me and [ ] to help you with the class? And does [ ] have one of these things?	9/2 @ 5:15pm - Email	
4	I don't understand my homework!!! Please call me!	9/2 @ 5:15pm - Call	
5	Call my daddy at [ ] he wants to speak to u	9/2 @ 5:20pm - Call	
6	Ms Magera, We have a family emergency on Tuesday and [ ] can't be at school. Please email me his homeowkr	9/2 @ 5:22pm - Email	
7	Hi ms magira I just want to say hi!	n/a	
8	Thank u for the I pad I love u! I love this class!	n/a	
9	Hey ms.magi era how are you doing? I want to know if I can get extra credit?	9/3 @ 4:15pm - Email	
10	How much money will tomorrow's field trip be?	9/3 @ 4:15pm - Email	
11	Ms magiera can you call my son needs help for tomorrow's test	9/3 @ 4:15pm - Call	
12	can you call me today because i need help with my homework over the phone.I don't understand stand the degrees. Can you let me stay after school to catch up on some work to get an a plus.	9/3 @ 4:22pm - Call	
13	i need tips how to learn more about how to make mixed numbers to fraction without yousing a caculater	9/3 @ 4:32pm - Email	
14	My plant is lost I had it in a window so it could grow but now it is lost.	class follow up	
15	You is best math teacher	n/a	
16	Dear Mrs.Mageria I couldn't understand yesterday math lesson.I didn't understand how you get the answer for it.After school today can I come and can you teach me how to figure it out?	class follow up	

Suggestion 3: Digital Newsletters/Class Blog

Class newsletters aren't a novel idea. As a new teacher, I tried sending home a class newsletter. At first, it was once a week, then once a month, and then, slowly, the practice died out. One reason is that these newsletters rarely made it home to the parents. I would regularly find them crumpled in students' backpacks or lockers. The other is that they were so time consuming to write.

Once my classroom entered its digital revolution, I had a chance to reinvent this strategy. Students began taking turns adding to a class blog. They wrote about things they were proud of and updates about our class. They included videos testimonials, photos from our learning, and examples of student work.

This role would rotate each week so that the blog could represent our entire class community, and the students would pair up to support one another in writing mechanics, ideas of what to share, and blogging best practices. Other students could submit ideas and links to digital content for the blog through a Google Form.

This was amazing because the heavy lifting of creating these newsletters was passed on to my students and also because they took more ownership in the story they wanted to tell. By giving the blog over to my students, they curated what about the class and week's learning was most important to them. Since they took pride in being the authors of these stories, they were avid ambassadors of the blog, encouraging family and friends to view it often.

Chapter 9

PLANNING FOR POWERFUL LEARNING

Ironically, I saved the chapter on planning for the very end of this section. If you've read this far and haven't found a problem of practice of your Teacher Innovation Exploration Plan (TIEP), perhaps this is where you need to be. Sometimes it's difficult to simply get started. How do you begin planning? Where can you find fresh ideas? How do you collaborate with your colleagues in a tightly packed school day schedule? This chapter digs into these questions and more while offering ideas for how to plan smarter and more collaboratively. A planning focus for your TIEP can be a pretty powerful one, as that is where the rest of your teaching—the differentiation, the assessment, and so on—comes from. Even creating a classroom environment requires thoughtful planning. So if you've yet to determine a problem of practice to dig into, not to fret—there are still more ideas yet to explore here!

PROBLEM: FINDING CURRICULAR RESOURCES

Creating engaging and developmentally appropriate instructional activities can be difficult when you have limited materials. However, introducing digital tools opens up a world of added resources. These resources are both varied in complexity and developmental level, and many are much more authentic than the textbooks in your cupboard. Check out a few of these suggestions for finding new curricular resources:

Suggestion 1: Pinterest and EduClipper

Pinterest is a resource for crafty holiday ideas and recipes. It's also chock full of classroom ideas, lesson plans, and activities. Simply type in your lesson topic or subject and watch as creative ideas pop up from educators around the world!

EduClipper is another amazing curation site, but this one was created by an educator, for education. Adam Bellow built this site not only for educators to find and share ideas and resources but for students as well. This is a very useful dashboard, as it's simple to use, easily connected to other social accounts, and populated by fellow edupeople. It also offers features that go far beyond Pinterest. For example, teachers can create classes and send specific boards of resources to their students as a whole class or through differentiated groups. Kids can collect and organize both public resources and their own digital content from cloud-based sites such as Google Drive and Dropbox as well as upload files from their computer to build digital portfolios, as we saw in Chapter 7.

Suggestion 2: Twitter and Google+

Some think that Twitter is simply a place for celebrities to share pictures of their sushi, and few think about Google+ at all. However, both social media sites are brimming with edufriends sharing instructional ideas. Simply search a hashtag like #kinderchat, #1stchat, or #mschat to find grade-level peers discussing ideas and sharing resources. These are spaces where you can find others

TOPIC	HASHTAG
English	#engchat
Science	#scichat
Math	#mathchat
Arts	#arted
Music	#musedchat
Social Studies	#sschat
Foreign Language	#langchat
History	#historyteacher
Physical Education	#physed
Connected Principals	#cpchat
Problem-Based Learning	#pblchat
Educational Technology	#edchat
Special Education	#spedchat
Getting Comments on Student Work	#Comments4Kids
Diversity and Equity in Education	#EduColor
Future Ready (Innovative Ideas Based on U.S. Department of Education Future Ready)	#FutureReady

to join you on your quest for innovation or perhaps check out their personal Innovation Islands. Check out some other popular education hashtags below.

Looking for even more educational hashtags? Check out the ever-updating list that Jerry Blumengarten (@cybraryman1) created at http://www.cybrary man.com/edhashtags.html.

Suggestion 3: Blogs!

There are also a myriad of blogs out there where educators just like you and me are trying, failing, iterating, and sharing. You can start with big-box sites such as Education Week or Edutopia to find regular bloggers and one-off articles on various education topics. Then a simple search engine query for "top education blogs" or "[fill in the blank grade level/subject/education topic] blog" will yield a ton of unexpected and amazing resources. I try my best to follow several blogs by subscribing to their updates. This way, I get an e-mail each time the author posts something new.

PROBLEM: SCHEDULING TIME FOR COLLABORATIVE TEAM PLANNING

A common challenge I ran into both as a classroom teacher and as a coach was finding time to collaboratively plan with my teams—not only grade-level partners but vertical alignment teams and integration with special education teachers, librarians, and the arts and physical education teachers. Some had to leave right after the final bell to pick up kids, others were tethered to a transportation schedule. Thankfully, I discovered a few tools help ease this burden:

Suggestion 1: Google Calendar

Google Calendar offers a bevy of scheduling tools. If everyone on your team is using Google Calendar with fidelity, you can use the "Find a Time" feature when creating events to determine a common open block to meet.

Suggestion 2: Doodle.com

If not everyone on your team is using Google Calendar, consider trying Doodle.com, a free tool that creates an availability survey. If you are feeling like splurging, you can upgrade to get full Google Calendar integration and have the tool overlay your existing schedule.

Suggestion 3: Google Hangouts

If you just can't find a time to meet together, try a virtual meeting! Google Hangouts is a free video-meeting platform that integrates other productivity tools such as Drive, YouTube, and sketching/visualization platforms. Teachers can gather from the convenience of their kitchen table, the comfort of their sofa, or while still in their classroom and plan collaboratively despite not being in the same place. Sometimes these meetings are even more productive as you aren't limited by a train schedule, day care pickup time, or simply the desire to get out of school.

PROBLEM: VERTICAL ALIGNMENT—WHAT'S THE REST OF THE SCHOOL TEACHING?

One year, my principal had themes that all teachers had to integrate into our lessons each month. One month, we were all focused on building our students' Tier 2 vocabulary. Another month, we were focusing on read-alouds and talking to the text. I really liked seeing how other grades were tackling these similar topics and their own unique developmental level. When these themes ended, I realized that I missed seeing what and how others were teaching. It became clear that while I thought I was really pushing my fourth graders, my lessons weren't really much more complex than the third grade teams'. I also gained a better insight as to what I needed to be preparing my students for in the next grade. Transparency in planning and teaching across grade levels helps create a more seamless experience for our students as they grow through our school. So how do you do this with little common planning time?

Additionally, each year you teach in the same content at the same grade level, things get a bit easier, not only because you have had practice with these learning objectives but also because you have already built lessons and now only need to tweak them rather than build them from scratch. However, what about new teachers? Or entire new teams? How do you archive unit and lesson plans and keep track of your school's unique curriculum?

Suggestion 1: Google Drive

Once again, Google Drive can be a handy tool in curating and saving content. In this case, consider creating folders for each grade level or subject. Teachers can add in their own lesson plans and view or make copies of previous plans. This makes it easier to see where students have been and where they are going. The revision history feature in Google Docs allows teachers to see how plans have changed over time and revert back to previous versions if need be.

If teachers want to take it a step forward, instead of merely adding in a Doc outlining the plan, create an entire folder for the unit plan within the grade level or subject folder. In this folder, teachers can include student work templates, rubrics, assessments, and so on. This makes it easier for use in other systems such as Google Classroom or an online learning management system.

Suggestion 2: Shared Calendars

To support this Google Drive collection, create shared teaching calendars. These calendars, when shared schoolwide, provide transparency across grade levels for what is being taught and when. Tip: Create a school-based Google account and use this to build all of the calendars (see Figure 9.1 and Figure 9.2). This way, if someone from your team moves on, you don't need to worry about regaining ownership of the calendar before they go. The master school account can create calendars for each grade level, subject, and even extracurricular events. What's nice about living in this ecosystem is that you can even attach the unit plans to the calendar events, making teaching and learning even more transparent throughout your building.

FIGURE 9.1 Google Calendar Entry

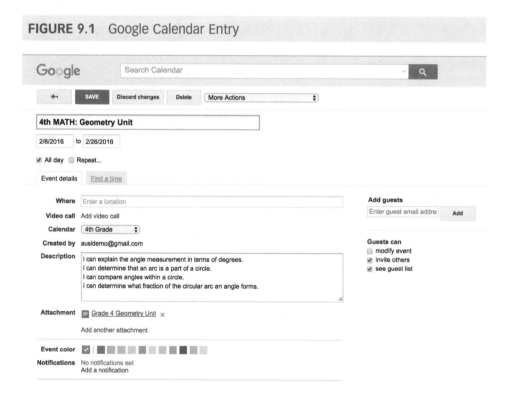

FIGURE 9.2   Google Calendar Month View

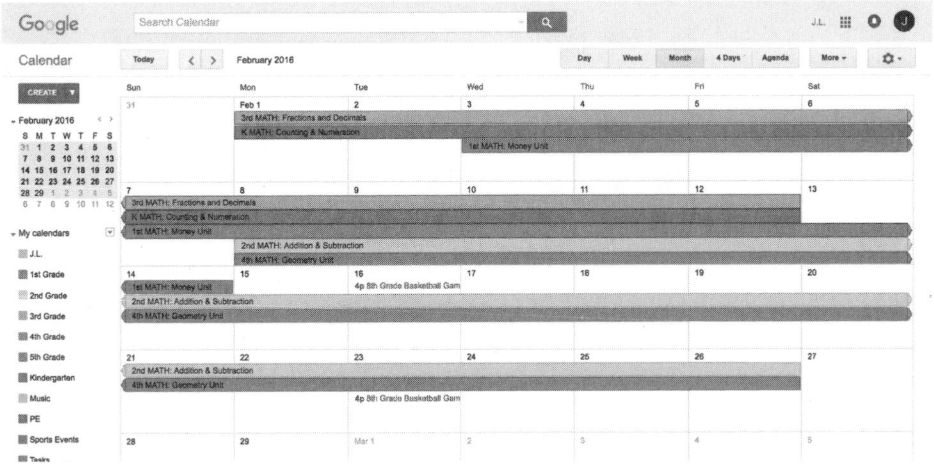

part III

SAILING INTO THE GREAT BEYOND

It takes courage to grow up and become who you really are.

—e. e. cummings

chapter 10

POWER TO THE PUPIL

Hopefully at this point, you've utilized your Teacher Innovation Exploration Plan (TIEP) to navigate around some of those nagging problems through creative use of your digital tools. If this is the case, you're ready to take advantage of your decreased mental and temporal workload to sail into deeper waters. If you are reading this book cover-to-cover and have yet to use your TIEP—think of this section as a preview for what you can do once you clear your plate of some of those nagging problems from Part II!

While embarking on the next leg of your transformation edventure may seem overwhelming, here's the good news: Once you've streamlined the foundational routines of your classroom, you get to take a break—it's time for the students to take the wheel. This section of the book is about taking the biggest leap of all—turning the keys of your classroom over to your students.

This is a huge course change for many. So much of our educational career is about planning for students, building supports for students, and creating systems so students don't have to guess what to do or when to do it. This section is about turning that thinking around and turning all of those decisions over to the kids. It's about challenging them to use their problem-solving and reasoning skills to consider these decisions and make positive choices.

Additionally, understand that this isn't a one-day journey. It takes some time and effort to build the needed skills and mindsets both in your students and yourself. First, we'll explore how to plan this sanctioned mutiny and then we'll explore how to empower students with voice. Then we'll dig into how they can use this newfound power for good.

Earlier in this book, I wrote about the moment when I was moved to change my practice and take more risks in my classroom. It was watching Sir Ken Robinson's seminal TED talk "Do Schools Kill Creativity?" This talk has been viewed over 28 million times and has spurred countless conversations about rethinking schools.

A main point of the "we need to change the way we think about school" movement is to empower students, to ask them not only what they want to learn but how they want to learn. Or even more, to give kids space to simply explore their own passions and interests and develop their own voices. But where should a teacher begin? It is one thing to be inspired to take a journey toward transforming your classroom and another thing completely to know which road to take. The first step is not only daunting but also a complete mystery to many. This first step for a number of schools isn't just about refreshing a lesson or correcting a strategy, it's completely changing the course of the pedagogy and mindset. Moreover, the teacher isn't the only one for whom this change might be difficult. As I learned the hard way, it also is a shift in practice for our students.

After I watched Sir Ken's talk, I decided to try out an innovative new idea called *20% time*. This is a concept coined by Google wherein employees have 20% of their work time to explore their own interests. When it was being explained to me, I thought, "Yes! This is exactly how I can start empowering my students and taking a first step toward changing my practice."

I spent weeks upon weeks thinking about how to roll this out and developing ideas for how to make this a reality. As I wrote in the previous chapter, it took me awhile to finally muster the courage to try it out. Finally, after pep talks from colleagues and lots of rewatching Sir Ken's speech, I took the leap. It was a Friday. I stood in front of my class and declared it "Do Whatever You Want Day." I set out engaging materials, curiosity-building questions, and challenges. I gave a speech about embracing wonder and setting your mind free. Then I told my students to begin exploring. And do you know what happened?

Absolutely nothing.

Instead of running wild and free with their imaginations and interests, my students froze. I asked one of my girls what she was waiting for and she replied, "A rubric."

I was too late. I had already become that teacher Sir Ken described in his TED talk—the one who killed creativity. I had broken my students and suffocated their wonder with anchor charts and checklists. They had become rubric zombies. Moreover, when I went to various colleagues to lament over this tragedy, they were happy to commiserate but unable to provide answers. "We don't have time to let our kids play all day," they said. "Innovation time like that, new-age practices, those are luxuries for charter schools. Schools like ours can't do things like this," they claimed. This was too much for me. I couldn't accept that student voice, empowerment, and freedom to explore wonder—the ability to allow our kids to be human—is a luxury for some schools.

Lucky for me, a friend and colleague had encouraged me to read a book with her—*Switch: How to Change Things When Change Is Hard* by Dan and Chip Heath. As we read it together, I was struck by one of its main ideas—bright spots. These are places where change is already happening organically. The concept is to find what makes this change work and apply it to the larger system so as to create more widespread change. I was relieved to find that my first step into innovation wasn't a total failure. I could go out, learn from others, and come back to take a second and third step . . . hopefully in a better direction. So I set off to discover some bright spots.

And I was able to find many places where innovation was happening both in the wild (students outside of schools) and in our classrooms. I talked with teachers, met students, and engaged parents to discover what made them special. In the end, I found three main lessons to instill in my practice:

1. **Cultivate curiosity.** The first thing that was evident to me was that our students had forgotten how to truly wonder. They had questions, but not the patience to follow their questions down a path to an unknown destination. I met many students and children along my journey who could ask a string of questions and end up on a wholly surprising and magical place of interest. However, in schools, student questions are often pushed to be about a certain focus or to gain more specific information, not simply for the sake of enjoying curiosity. They had forgotten how to wonder. To help my students dig into their passions, I needed to remind them how to follow that yellow brick road of "what if" and "I wonder" to wherever it may take them.

2. **Outwit obstacles.** My students were quitters. I hate to say it, but at the time of this exploration, I found that even when engaged in something that truly mattered to them, once they hit an obstacle, they got frustrated and wanted to give up. When in search for bright spots, one of the shining examples I found was that the children in transformative classrooms had built a resilience to failure and problems. Instead of feeling helpless, they learned to outwit these obstacles, even to see through them. This is a skill that must be built up in our students before they can truly be empowered.

3. **Purposeful playtime.** I had been allowing for playtime, but this playtime was short and rationed out. I began to discover that we need to allow our students more time to play, experiment, fail, and dig in. I learned that when students first were able to focus their curiosity to a specific interest and build problem-solving skills, they then needed ample, unstructured playtime to get lost in their exploration. If given enough time, this play becomes purposeful. The result is student creations and student self-empowerment.

I've begun to implement these tenets into my work with students and teachers. While it's not easy to turn the ship around, it's an important task. Schools might be killing creativity, but that doesn't mean it's too late to change this. All it takes is that first step. In this chapter, we will dig into these three lessons to learn how to increase student voice, choice, and creativity.

CULTIVATE CURIOSITY: HOW DO I BUILD CURIOSITY?

Once you know to cultivate curiosity, how do you do this within your classroom? How do you get students to understand the difference between various types of questions and dig deeper into their own innate sense of curiosity and wonder?

First students need to relearn the art of asking a question. Many of our students are adept at asking clarifying questions: Who? What? Where? When? Why? How? Oftentimes, we focus on the *why* and *how* as deeper-level questions. These clarifying questions are usually what are frequently referred to as "Googleable questions" (i.e., I could hop on an Internet search engine and find the answer to this question). They include the following:

- Who founded Facebook?
- What is the capital of Iowa?
- Where is the largest ball of yarn in the world?
- When is the lunar eclipse?
- Why do dogs wag their tails?
- How do planes fly?

But it's not that easy to say, "All questions that start with _____ are Googleable." For example, the following questions start with the same words but don't have a single answer:

- Who is the best presidential candidate for teachers?
- What can I do to help improve my community?
- Where will the next tornado touch down?
- When will the polar ice caps melt?
- Why should I stop using Facebook?
- How can we stop gun violence?

Sorting Your Questions: Questdones and Questruns

Although Googleable questions may come from a real place of curiosity, that wonder is ended once the search results are returned. We called these *Questdones*—you ask the question, you get the answer, you're done. Instead, try getting your students to ask questions that don't have one answer. I call these *Questruns* because these questions often turn into a quest as there is no simple answer (Figure 10.1). You have to investigate, analyze, and make your own meaning.

To get your students to ask these Questruns, give them practice sorting their questions into Questdones and Questruns. Start by sharing a wonder catalyst—a quote, image, or video (some of my favorite sources to find these can be found in

FIGURE 10.1 Questdones and Questruns

Questdones	**Questruns**

Questions that have a finite answer. Usually these questions can be answered by performing an Internet search or referencing another trusted source. Once the reference is checked, the answer is **done.**

Questions that don't have a finite answer. These questions cannot be answered by performing an Internet search. To answer these questions, you must **analyze, evaluate,** and **offer opinion.**

Examples:

- Who are the presidential candidates?
- What is a community?
- Where do tornadoes occur?
- When was the ice age?
- Why do I have to be 13 to sign up for Facebook?
- How do planes fly?

Examples:

- Who is the best presidential candidate for teachers?
- What can I do to help improve my community?
- Where will the next tornado touch down?
- When will the polar ice caps melt?
- Why should I be careful when using Facebook?
- How can we build faster planes?

Webb's Depth of knowledge Levels

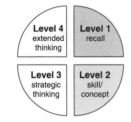

Webb's Depth of knowledge Levels

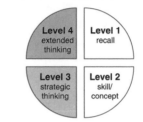

Bloom's Taxonomy Levels

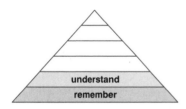

Bloom's Taxonomy Levels

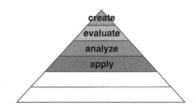

the table below). Once you select your wonder catalyst, throw it up on a screen, share it through your learning management system (LMS) or insert it into a document. Then have students ask any and all questions. They can do this on Post-its, a backchannel, a discussion stream, in a Google Doc—it doesn't matter as long as it's free-form and open.

It's important that at this stage, students don't audit their questioning. Don't ask them to try for Questruns yet—just have them pour out all the questions that come to mind. After they've had some time to think of questions, ask them to add a few more, but this time with a mindset of "what if." As they examine the wonder catalyst—the picture, the video, the quote—ask them to wonder "What if?" possibilities to frame their questions and see how this changes the number of Questdones and Questruns.

For example, when I showed the image below (Figure 10.2) to my class, here are some of the questions that came up:

FIGURE 10.2 United Screen

- Is the computer sideways, too?
- How did they do that?
- Can you fill a plane with water and make a giant pool inside and it would still fly?
- How many flights are on that screen?
- Why are the other two screens blank?
- Do airplanes destroy our planet with jet fuel?
- If I filled my dad's car with jet fuel, what would happen?
- What airport is this?
- How long would it take to fly all of those flights?
- How much did it cost for all of those people to buy flights?
- Is there a better way to travel than flying?

When I asked them to apply a filter of "what if" to the question, see how their questions changed. (Note: This is not requiring the use of a sentence stem. The questions could start with any words. I just asked my students to consider unconsidered possibilities and then ask those questions.)

- I wonder if the planes are flying sideways, too. Can they do that?
- What if you had eyes that were vertical, would you see sideways?
- What if turning the screen showed places in another dimension?

- I wonder if humans could turn their necks sideways like birds if we could do more stuff like read sideways easier.
- How could we create better airport information boards?
- How can we make flying easier and less boring?

Note that many more of their questions don't have finite answers. These are the type of curiosity builders that inspire our students to dig deeper and discover new and enticing challenges to solve.

WONDER CONTENT	DESCRIPTION	LINK
101Qs	This site, created by Dan Meyer, simply has one piece of media (an intriguing photo or video) per page. At the bottom of each page, it invites viewers to ask the questions that come to mind. That's it—a curiosity builder!	http://www.101qs.com
Google Earth View	Google Earth View is a collection of incredible satellite images of our planet from space. I like the Google Earth extension for Google Chrome to start the day off with students. This extension changes the new tab page so that instead of the stock Google Search landing page, you get a different zoomed-in satellite image. The beauty is that not all are recognizable. Some are rocky faces of a mountain that look more like the surface of an ocean. Others are gorgeous views of cities that strike wonder at the architecture and angles. Various questions are instigated about mathematics, anthropology, history, culture, science, and more all from these satellite images. Oh—and they are all clickable, so you can go to the interactive version to see what's around that image and where it is on earth!	http://bit.ly/googleearthview
Student-Built Wonder Decks	Ask students to find images that interest them or could incite wonder. Take photos of them and add them to a Google Slide deck. Allow other students to add comments to the deck to ask questions.	http://drive.google.com

OUTWIT OBSTACLES: HOW DO I TEACH PERSEVERANCE?

Once your students have a juicy question to investigate, it's time to dig in and try to find answers. However, too often, our students give up at the first sign of trouble. It's important to teach them perseverance and reset their mindset to be solutions focused. Just as you spent some time throughout the previous chapters identifying and addressing problems with creative solutions, so must your students. I often begin by building their tolerance to failure.

In Chapter 5, I described the #FailFest. This is a way to help your students begin to outwit obstacles. They need to see them as challenges to pass through, not obstacles blocking their way. Set up a community culture of embracing and celebrating failure and a system to reflect on next steps to learn from that failure. Hopefully through this process, you can support your students in moving from that First Attempt In Learning to an improved Second Attempt In Learning—from FAILing to SAILing.

Building Rube Goldberg machines allows students to practice failure and iteration. If you can't picture these contraptions, think back to your childhood when you played Mouse Trap. A Rube Goldberg machine is a series of simple machines or mechanisms set together so that one action sets off a chain reaction to accomplish an ultimate task, such as capturing a mouse or turning off a light. You can get your kids excited about this challenge by watching the music video for the OK Go song *This Too Shall Pass* (scan QR Code 10.1 for the link to video). The song itself is catchy, but it's the almost four-minute-long Rube Goldberg machine that the video follows that is mesmerizing. Once you've got your students ready to rock some Rube Goldberg machines, give them all a simple task—like putting a marble into cup—and see which team can do so in exactly 21 steps. (The 21 steps is arbitrary; you can make this number higher or lower, depending on how difficult you want to make the challenge.) The important piece of this—besides having fun, creating, and problem solving—is teaching your students to consistently narrate frustration. What didn't work? Why didn't it work? What can you learn from that failure? How can you improve on the next iteration?

QR Code 10

Another video to watch is Audri's Monster Trap (scan QR Code 10.2 to watch). In this video, a young engineer decides to create a Rube Goldberg machine (Fun fact: He was inspired to create this machine after seeing the OK Go video!). The beauty is that he knows that he won't succeed in the first try. He predicts "umpteen failures" and is delighted to find that he *only failed three times*! While his exuberance at failing forward is a powerful example for our students, I also ask them to pause the video and reflect on what Audri changed from one take to another. Did he move something? Did he shorten something? Did he add or take away something? Why was his subsequent trial more successful than the one preceding it?

QR Code 10

Throughout these activities, it is vital that students reflect. They can do this through a blog, either written or video. (I prefer a hybrid blog where students both write out their thinking and also create video testimonials and post artifacts to support their reflection.) Regardless of how they capture their reflections, they should be asking themselves:

- What obstacles did I find today?
- How did I respond to those obstacles?
- What did I learn from that experience?
- What will I do differently next time?

They should also follow up on these blog posts to share how they reacted differently if/when they encounter the same obstacle in the future or how they navigated around it.

These FAIL-to-SAIL blogs impact not only academic learning but social-emotional reactions as well. After all, our students are not only encountering challenges in their studies but in their interactions with others as well. If your students are regularly reflecting on how they outwit obstacles by celebrating failure and sharing iteration, your learning culture will shift toward one where students are ready to power up and begin to drive their own learning vehicles.

These blogs should also be shared with parents. Encouraging failure is incredibly uncomfortable for many teachers, but it can be even more so for parents. Ease them into the concept by creating these blogs ahead of time to show that the focus isn't really the failure but the learning from mistakes and ability to take risks. If a parent is unclear on the *why* behind this and you want to know more about how to talk to them about the power of failure, or even give them the resources to read for themselves, check out *The Gift of Failure: How the Best Parents Learn to Let Go So Their Children Can Succeed* by Jessica Lahey.

OK Go—Get Inspired

You may already be a fan of OK Go—if not, perhaps you may recall them from their iconic 2009 treadmill video. I have been a long-term diehard fan of this band for many reasons—hometown love as they're #ChiTown locals, their heartwarming start as fifth graders in camp, and, most powerfully, the impact they've had on my students. In past years, OK Go has become one of the most inspiring catalysts for my kids' learning. Let me tell you why.

First off, the adorable story behind how this band started: As 11-year-olds, lead singer Damien Kulash and bassist Tim Norwind met at Interlochen Arts Camp. They met, fell in bro-love, and kept in touch after camp, sharing mixtapes and ideas. The name of the band came from their camp art teacher, who would say to them "OK. . . . Go!" How lovely and telling that these two children found each other in an environment where they could truly be themselves and have the space to play. Also inspiring is that they chose the name of their band based on those simple two words: OK Go. Go play. Go explore. Go get messy.

Quick meta-tangent: How often do we as teachers simply say to our students, "OK. . . . Go!" And when we do finally release them to an activity, how free are they really to truly "go"? What parameters have we set that may limit their "go"? Have we set up an environment where they feel it's really "OK"?

Ah, now we're back from that meta-tangent, let's get into how OK Go can inspire your students. Many of their videos are models of STEAM. Below are some of my favorite videos and how you might use them in your classroom.

VIDEO	PREMISE	SUBJECTS	IDEAS FOR USE
This Too Shall Pass http://goo.gl/qwCSK	Giant Rube Goldberg machine timed to the beat of the song	Math Science Art Music	As you discussed elsewhere in this chapter, this video features a giant Rube Goldberg machine that is timed out to the beat of the song. It teaches students perseverance and iteration as well as many topics in math and science. There are cause-and-effect relationships, various laws of physics in action, and lots of excellent rate and timing challenges to discuss in mathematics. The video is also teeming with colors, shapes, and patterns to bring art into the investigation.
Needing/Getting http://goo.gl/HGDlo	A giant musical instrument built out of found sounds, engineered to create percussion in the song	Math Science Music	This is a glorious celebration of "found sounds" to create music. Driving a car through a musical obstacle course in the middle of the desert, the band members create the percussion to back their vocals. Challenge your students to find rhythms in their own school day, taking notes about sounds (i.e., moving carts down the hall to provide bass or girls playing Double Dutch to add the beat). To engineer a machine that will create all of these sounds, students need to consider rates and timing. To create the different tones and sounds needed, students need to think about the physics of sound and sound waves.
I Won't Let You Down http://goo.gl/TOF47k	Synchronized dancing/driving on a massive scale and recorded in half time to create visual effects	Math Science Social Studies Art Music Social Emotional Learning	This video's explosion of patterns, rates, and shapes can inspire your students to dig into the math of music. Prompt them to explore marching band patterns books to find the mathematics in planning something of this scale. Compare the real-time speed video to the finished product and how filming in half time supported the ultimate effect. Explore the timing and rates involved as well as lines and trajectories the dancers had to learn to create the patterns. Additionally, this video can prompt kids to reflect on teamwork. Ask your students to consider the patience and teamwork required to

(Continued)

VIDEO	PREMISE	SUBJECTS	IDEAS FOR USE
			coordinate such synchronized choreography. As my class studied this video, one of my students commented, "I really wonder how they all got along so well. Sometimes we can't even line up for lunch; how can we get everyone in our class to team up to do this?" We spent a good 15–20 minutes seeing if we could cooperate enough to time a jumping photo first in the hall, then moving to the classroom as we realized we needed to literally sit down and think before we jumped.
			There is also a social studies link to this video as it was filmed entirely in Japan. It is interesting for students to think about the culture of the schools there, why they are in uniform, and whether this video represents any other aspects of Japanese culture.
The Writing's on the Wall http://goo.gl/VJSa2n	Series of shapes, patterns, and colors paired with dynamic camera angles to create optical illusions	Math Science Art Music	This video is a wonderland of optical illusions and awesome for teaching about light, reflection, and refraction. As with all of the other videos, there are mathematical themes of rate and timing as well, but this one also digs into geometric shapes and angles. Students may wonder how certain angles and shapes created these illusions.
Here It Goes Again http://goo.gl/ukVDU	Dancing on four treadmills to the beat of the song, creating timed choreography	Math Science Music Physical Education	OK Go's first breakout video was also its simplest: using the rate of four treadmills to create a dynamic dance floor. This is certainly a "don't try this at home" type video, but it is interesting to ask students how different variables would have changed the video. What if the rate of one of the treadmills had been changed? What would that have done?

Note: Hoping to get some English/language arts action in there as well? Have students transcribe the lyrics and look for patterns in rhyming, alliteration, syntax, and so on.

Ask them to find metaphors, similes, and other figurative language. Challenge them to rewrite the lyrics using different metaphors or regarding a different topic.

OK Go's innovative music and music videos have not only engaged my students in my own learning goals but also pushed them to wonder and explore ideas neither they nor I had considered before. OK Go—you may entertain millions of people with your snappy beats, but you're making a real difference in the lives of these students by daring to be different and thinking outside of the box. Thank you for innovating, and to your Interlochen Art Teacher—thank you for saying "OK. . . . Go!"

PURPOSEFUL PLAYTIME: HOW DO I FIND THE TIME FOR PURPOSEFUL PLAY?

Once your students have internalized a resilient and "yes I can" mindset, they need time to play and explore. They should take their new ability to outwit obstacles and explore and investigate the Questruns they discovered as they cultivated their curiosity.

This time should be as unstructured as possible. It's an open time to explore and play with their wonder-inducing Questrun. Some students thrive with a tad of structure, so giving choices can help those who need a starting place.

When creating choices—whether it be choice boards, activity selections, or options in your LMS—note that choices are not all created equal. Sometimes giving students too-limited options isn't much better than dictating exactly what they should do. To help build more holistic choice, break down student agency into four component parts: process, content, product, and environment. Engage students in conversation about their level of choice in each of these areas. Reflect on the following questions to help you consider whether your choice time is about actual agency or the illusion of choice.

What choice do the students have in determining

- the design of their learning experience? (process)
- their learning content/resources? (content)
- how they show/synthesize their learning? (product)
- where they explore/learn/build? (environment)

Once you've determined how to scaffold choice, the next consideration is how to find time for unstructured playtime in an already-too-short school day scheduled beyond available hours. Here are three creative scheduling ideas, listed from most scaffolded to most open. Try a few on for size and see which one best fits your situation and needs.

Reimagined Centers

Centers aren't a new concept. However, they are often considered an elementary-age concept and are most often highly structured. Try reimagining these as pockets of time. When students are at the "teacher center" or working on a required extra practice/support assignment, try retooling the other centers in a free-exploration time. Let's say you have 30 minutes for center time during the day, or you're a middle school or high school teacher with 30 minutes of work time during your period. Perhaps you break your students into three groups, and each visit your center for 10 minutes to get face-to-face instruction. The remaining 20 minutes are left up to them to tinker, play, and explore.

20% Time

Genius hour or *20% time* is the concept of designating a regular time during the school day or week where students are given free reign over what they learn, how they learn it, and what end products they create. This is the perfect way for them to dig into their Questruns and pursue their curiosity. Most often, these periods are preset—one day a week or one hour a day or even one hour a week. The students are supported through conferencing and focusing prompts. It is truly a workshop model, where each student follows his or her own interests or ideas and the teacher serves as a support system. To dig into this idea, I highly recommend the book *The 20Time Project* by Kevin Brookhouser.

Open Scheduling

I first saw this concept at Taupaki School just outside of Auckland, New Zealand. Students had their own individual learning plans (see the example in Figure 10.3) where they self-schedule what and when they'll tackle learning goals. The teacher began the year by filling in the "must do" tasks, and the remainder of the day is up to the students to fill in with their interests or needs. Teams of teachers came together to offer core content lessons in block scheduling—an advanced math lesson, a literacy group, a science investigation. Those times were blocked onto the schedule for students who need it and given as options for others to join should they so decide. As the year progressed, students got more and more blocks of time where they could determine their own activities and learning. Students reviewed their learning by highlighting their schedule green, yellow, or red based on how well they think they did during that block and whether they think they could have put in more effort.

The thing that truly struck me about this was that none of these things were happening during a designated time. There wasn't a specific genius hour or part of the day that students could dig into this powerful agency and practice this choice. It was part of the fabric of how the school works. Students were given a choice, they explored freely, and it works. Classrooms were constantly littered in hot glue guns, various laptops, and popsicle sticks. Barefoot children sat in beanbags in the grass and read to each other. This was just how they do school. Every day.

FIGURE 10.3 School Schedule

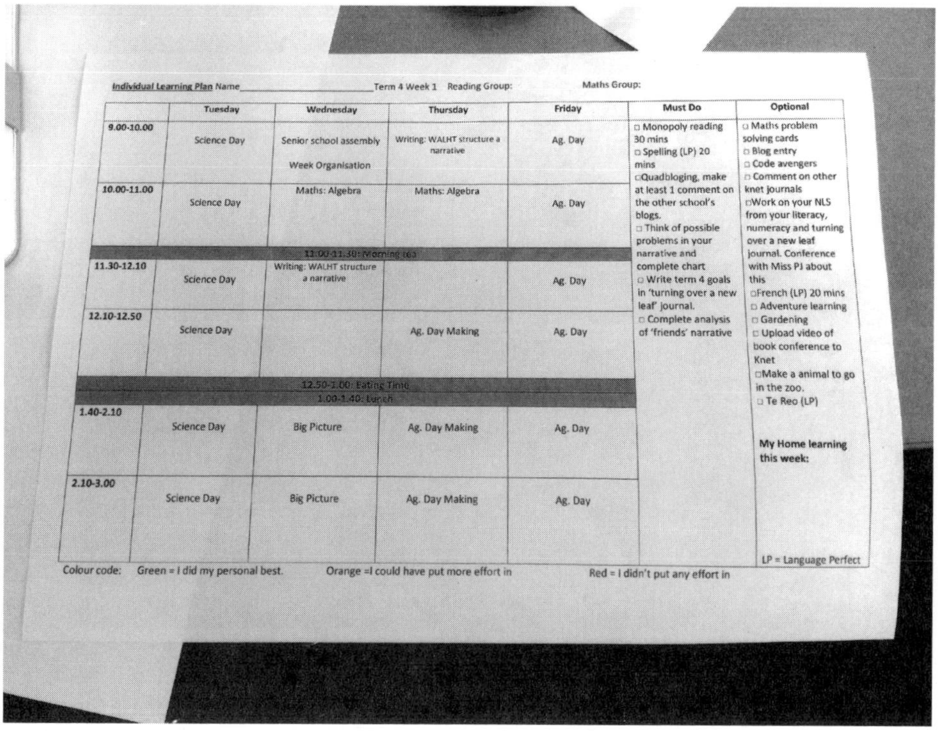

Individual Learning Plan Name________________ Term 4 Week 1 Reading Group: Maths Group:

	Tuesday	Wednesday	Thursday	Friday	Must Do	Optional
9.00-10.00	Science Day	Senior school assembly Week Organisation	Writing: WALHT structure a narrative	Ag. Day	□ Monopoly reading 30 mins □ Spelling (LP) 20 mins □Quadbloging, make at least 1 comment on the other school's blogs. □ Think of possible problems in your narrative and complete chart □ Write term 4 goals in 'turning over a new leaf' journal. □ Complete analysis of 'friends' narrative	□ Maths problem solving cards □ Blog entry □ Code avengers □ Comment on other knet journals □Work on your NLS from your literacy, numeracy and turning over a new leaf journal. Conference with Miss PJ about this □French (LP) 20 mins □ Adventure learning □ Gardening □ Upload video of book conference to Knet □Make a animal to go in the zoo. □ Te Reo (LP) **My Home learning this week:** LP = Language Perfect
10.00-11.00	Science Day	Maths: Algebra	Maths: Algebra	Ag. Day		
11.00-11.30: Morning tea						
11.30-12.10	Science Day	Writing: WALHT structure a narrative		Ag. Day		
12.10-12.50	Science Day		Ag. Day Making	Ag. Day		
12.50-1.00: Eating Time						
1.00-1.40: Lunch						
1.40-2.10	Science Day	Big Picture	Ag. Day Making	Ag. Day		
2.10-3.00	Science Day	Big Picture	Ag. Day Making	Ag. Day		

Colour code: Green = I did my personal best. Orange =I could have put more effort in Red = I didn't put any effort in

SOURCE: Stephen Lethbridge.

Bringing the Purpose to the Playtime: Entering Creation Station

No matter how you schedule the playtime, to help make it purposeful, challenge students to create something from their curiosity. Encourage tinkering not only to build resilience in your students but also to exercise their ability to create. To facilitate this, you may want to transform your classroom into a MakerSpace.

A MakerSpace is simply a learning area dedicated to creation. MakerSpaces are often stocked with tools and materials students can use to tinker, design, build, and explore. To start, gather the tools and supplies. You can do this with little or even no budget. Work with your local appliance stores, school custodial staff, and community to collect cardboard, Styrofoam, plastics, and

FIGURE 10.4 Students Exploring Materials

other intriguing materials. Invest a small amount of money in hot glue guns, safety scissors, string, rubber bands, and a variety of tapes. If you have an actual budget, consider springing for a 3D printer or robotics.

If you don't have a ton of space in your classroom, ask each student to bring in a shoebox. Give them the parameter that they can tinker and explore as much and as wildly as they desire during their playtime/maketime/tinkertime. However, at the end of the period, their creation and all of its materials must fit back into that box. It adds another layer of challenge for them to problem solve around but also allows you to create a workshop in your classroom when you don't have built-in storage.

If the cost or space is still an obstacle, don't worry; you don't need to get fancy to create the MakerSpace. In fact, the *Space* in MakerSpace is a bit of a misnomer. It's really more about the mindset than the materials. Encourage your students to ask questions and use their hands and imagination to answer them (see Figure 10.4). Allow them to get messy, to get loud. As with any workshop model, facilitate often but always remember to guide from the side, not lead from the front. Ask lots of questions, but make sure it's the students giving answers, not you. Help them stay focused on their original Questrun of curiosity, but if their wonder wanders in a different direction, support that as well. Be patient with their process and know that unlike traditional units of study, each student's exploration cycle will happen on its own course and time. For example, one of my students started off asking questions about patents, specifically how an iPhone was different from an Android phone. After some investigation, this pivoted into inventing his own top secret device (see Figure 10.5). Ultimately, his learning and creation evolved into something more complex and powerful than his original goal. So provide safe spaces for students to store their creations mid-process.

FIGURE 10.5 Top Secret Project

Reflect, Reflect, Reflect

And throughout all of this, don't forget about our constant companion in student-centered learning—reflection. Make sure your students are evaluating their own journey, auditing their choices, and considering how to be more productive the next day. This can be done formally through a blog or reflection form or informally through discussions.

Also, encourage students to bring home their ideas and thinking to share with their families. I was so excited to hear from one parent that as we delved deeper into purposeful playtime, she began changing the daily question she asked her daughter when she walked in the door. Instead of asking, "What did you learn today?" to which she usually received a "I don't know" or "Nothing," she started asking, "What did you *create* today?" This resulted in excited chatter about Questruns and "Did you know . . .?", hinges and screws, and ideas and iterations.

As you build the culture of student agency in your classroom, the next step is to help students look within and find their own unique perspective. What are they passionate about? What messages do they have to share? How would they share it if they could? In the next chapter, we'll explore how to help students harness their newfound power.

Chapter 11

Discovering the Power of Voice

For a long time, I joked that a teacher's favorite two letters to use in the classroom were *N* and *O*. As I spent more time in the classroom, I realized that they might actually be *S* and *H*—as in *Shhhhhh*. I spent so much time *Sh*-ing rogue conversations during silent reading, chatter in the hallway, and the whole class when the decibel level rose too high during work time. It became such a prevalent habit that one day after class, I *Sh*-ed the El train as it rattled past my classroom window. I knew I was focusing too much on silencing my students, but I told myself that all of those *Sh*s were serving the greater purpose of classroom management. However, if I was honest with myself, I had to admit that *Sh* was really just short for *Sh*-ut up. And really, was shutting up my students helping at all?

AMPLIFYING OUR STUDENTS

When committing to support student agency, an essential piece is amplifying student voice. Once you've begun to allow your students to captain the ship, they need this strong voice to share their ideas and discuss their own adventures. Amplifying our students isn't a simple task. Beyond putting a kibosh on all the *Sh*-ing, we need to also teach the students how to find what they want to say, recognize the power in their words, and learn how to use that power for good. Once the teacher releases student voices from their *Sh*-cage, they won't magically float back into the students' windpipes and allow them to sing out mid-melody like Ariel in *The Little Mermaid*. We have to scaffold this reintroduction.

First off, set some goals what you hope to accomplish. Here are some common goals:

- Cultivating student voice and helping them find what they want to say

  - How to find the right messages for the right audiences
  - How to share your opinion without degrading others
  - How to send a message clearly and succinctly

FIGURE 11.1 Student Working on Laptop

- ○ How to determine if your message is something you'd like to remain a part of your permanent digital footprint
- Connecting students with an authentic audience of peers and experts
  - ○ Using social media to amplify your reach
  - ○ Using blogs, video conferencing tools, and digital networks to establish learning connections
  - ○ Collecting and learning from audience feedback
- Promoting introverted students' participation and extroverted students' collaboration
  - ○ Trying various pathways to share thoughts
  - ○ Learning how to respond to and converse with others versus one-way communication
  - ○ Determining whether your message adds value

Next, map out the journey to guide your students toward these goals. Below is a stairstepped approach I like to follow. It begins with finding their inner voices and slowly opens their circle of sharing outward before ultimately reaching a global audience (Figure 11.1).

STEP 1: FINDING THEIR
INNER VOICE—BLOGS VERSUS DIARIES

Start off with daily blogging. Give each student his or her own blog as well as prompts each day to reflect upon. The prompts can be as narrow or open as you determine, but allow free flow of ideas and don't focus too heavily on specific writing conventions at first. This is practice for them to decide what to say and how to say it and to reflect on learning, wondering, and/or life experiences. If you're concerned about the whole wide world seeing your students' thoughts and messages before they have had a chance to try out their voices, try out moderated blog sites such as Kidblog.org. Platforms like this allow students to blog in a safe environment behind a garden wall. The teacher can lock the blog down to the class itself or open it in increments to certain individuals (such as families or peers) or entire partner classes. The teacher can moderate the content and feedback tools that are available as well.

Regardless of the blogging platform you select, make sure you give students time to read each other's writing and respond to it. The power of a blog is its audience. The audience can provide feedback and someone to whom the student can write their message. The audience pushes students to make their writing more dynamic and helps prompt them to think more carefully about their message. So make sure that no matter the blog format you use, you ensure that people are reading and responding on a regular basis. After all, a blog that no one reads is just a diary.

To build an audience, there are many options. The most insular is assigning student Critical Friend triads. These peers are given time on a weekly basis to read and respond to one another's blogs. Usually, teachers ask the triads to start with their two partners and then, if time allows, move on to respond to others in their class. This way, each student receives at least two comments per week and possibly more.

If you want to move beyond the walls of your room, consider partnering with other classes either within or beyond your school. Find colleagues who are exploring blogging and create Critical Friend triads or quartets across your classrooms. One website that offers to make these matches for you is Quadblogging.net. They will connect you with three other classrooms from across the world, teaming you all up to read and comment on one another's blogs. Each week, one class is featured and the other three provide comments. This allows for less frequent feedback, as your students would only be featured once a month, but the quantity and diversity of that feedback would be increased.

Another, much more open method of building an audience for your students is tweeting their blog posts to the world. This is the most daring approach, as it moves completely beyond the garden wall. A popular hashtag, #comments4kids, is used often by teachers to garner responses from other educators on their students' work. While I have never personally seen this hashtag used for evil, I would suggest that you request parent permission before sharing student blogs in this more public way.

In 2012, the Chicago Teachers Union went on strike. Regardless of the opinions and politics around this event, one thing was clear to me: how this was affecting my students. As it goes in situations when adults are in conflict, children oftentimes blame themselves. I wanted to make sure they understood why the strike was happening, how this was in support of students, and that they weren't at fault in any way. As my students began to learn more about unions, strikes, and school systems, they became more and more interested in gobbling up any and all news coverage on the current events arising in their city and school.

As the eve of the strike approached, one of sixth graders (blog alias "TECHViBE") asked if she could still blog even though she wasn't at school. I told her, "Of course, it's your blog. Just remember what we learned about only writing what you feel best represents yourself and your thinking as a scholar and citizen." She agreed and went on with her day. Three days into the strike, I had forgotten about this conversation until I received an e-mail from KidBlog, saying that she had a new post (Figure 11.2). I read it and was amazed by this student's candor and insight. As I had previous permission from her mother, I tweeted her post. Within a few hours, she had accrued dozens of comments from educators, local talking heads, and other community members.

FIGURE 11.2   Tweet

While I was impressed with how far this young lady had come in her ability to craft a message, state it eloquently, and share it with the world, I was even more amazed by how thoughtfully she responded to the many commenters. Below are a few of the comments and interactions from this post:

(Guest Commenter) September 13, 2012 at 1:16 PM

> I think the president can't get behind either side of the issue without looking bad—after all, he was buddies with Rahm (he was his Chief of Staff), but I'm pretty sure he's personally pro-union. So he can't back one side without upsetting the other. I agree 100% with you though

FIGURE 11.3 Student Innovation Team » TECHViBE During the Strike

TECHViBE During the Strike

Categories: Blog
September 13, 2012 @ 12:32 PM   30 Comments

Hi world,

TECHViBE is back. So as you all know all of Chicago Public Schools are on strike. I go to a Chicago Public School. This strike is really upsetting me. I feel like people aren't respecting my teachers who work so hard. I think that if the mayor wants teachers to work more hours and have more than 30 students in a class then he is going to have raise their pay. This is the first time in years that we have gone on strike. Can't they agree on making schools better?

And I think this is the worst time to get on strike because progress reports were supposed to come out this Friday! I don't they are still going to give it to us because teachers haven't been putting grades in for anything for half a school week and I believe the strike is going to be going on for much longer.

My teachers said that for all the days we miss we might get the days back at the end of the year. OK, but that means that all the learning we were supposed to learn during this time period is going to be taught to us at the end of the year - and it will be too late for ISAT.

I think that the teachers are doing the right thing because we deserve more and they deserve more. Also teachers have to stay after school, buy supplies for the class, and much more. My teachers haven't complained, not once, but now that they want to put more students in a class and make school days longer........ they're pushing it to the limit. This is not looking good for the president or the mayor because if teachers are going on strike and the reelections are coming up then people will think that he is the cause for their children not going to school.

I think that the president knows what the people want so how about he talks to the mayor about making this right. Why doesn't he come out and help? I support my teachers. But let's hope that this strike will end soon.

TECHViBE out.

(Continued)

(Continued)

TECHViBE September 16, 2012 at 6:21 PM

I agree, but he needs to choose his career or his friend.

(Guest Commenter) September 14, 2012 at 5:20 PM

I feel so much pride in knowing you are a student of Chicago's Public Schools. I am excited about the opinions you have about other historical events that affect us as times go on. I can't wait to see how this blog grows with you as you make choices for your personal future. Thank you for being on our side. We're very lucky. And, yes, I'd love to read about connections you made to what you learned about equity and education from last year's Museum Walk!

TECHViBE September 17, 2012 at 11:03 AM

Thank you for reading my blog and I just might write a post about equity and equality because that gives me a great idea.

Not only did this turn out to be a powerful social justice, history, and writing lesson for this student, but it was eye-opening for me as well. Here was the proof in the pudding: If we equip our students with the tools and strategies to find and use their voices, their power and impact can be limitless. I returned from the strike renewed in so many ways—one of which caused me to want to find a way to take this student empowerment and amplify it (see Figure 11.3 and this QR Code).

goo.gl/yV1yQ5

STEP 2: SHARING THEIR VOICE WITH OTHERS—BUILDING CLASSROOM DISCUSSIONS AND BACKCHANNELING

Once you've ignited that spark to share and speak out through daily reflection and blogging, next begin to develop your students' ability to bring others into that conversation. For some of our students, finding something to say and saying it isn't the difficult part—it's learning how to *listen and respond* that poses the toughest challenge. It is also valuable for students to know how to react productively when someone disagrees or critiques their ideas or opinions. This is an integral skill when interacting in a more open forum such as discussion walls or social media. So before releasing your students into the world of social media, it's important to practice in a walled garden first.

I like to begin by helping my students see the issue and need for equity of voice in discussions. I seat the class in a circle, facing in. I draw this circle on a sheet of paper and write each student's name down according to their seat. I then ask the students a discussion question and each time someone speaks, I draw a line to their seat. When someone else speaks, I draw a line from the first speaker to the next and so on. At the end of the conversation, I share the drawing. Oftentimes, it looks like this (Figure 11.4):

FIGURE 11.4 Student Conversations With Teacher

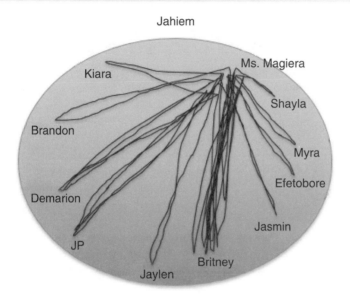

Notice that all of the lines of conversation start and end with me, the teacher. A few students spoke the majority of the time with the conversation being ping-ponged back and forth to the teacher. One student never spoke, while others had a few moments here and there. A healthy conversation should have more cross-student interaction, full participation, and less connection back to the teacher. It should look more like a spider web (see Figure 11.5):

If you want to dig in deeper and get more granular with this process, consider video recording the conversation as well. Then rewatch the video as a class and ask students to code their contributions as:

- N = new idea
- AR = affirmative response
- CR = constructive or critical response
- CQ = clarifying question
- NQ = new question

FIGURE 11.5   Students Interacting With Other Students and Teacher

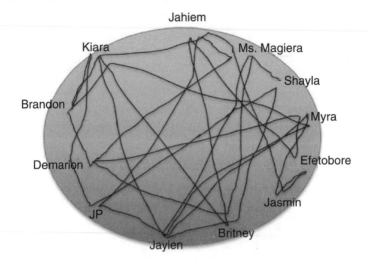

The most common pattern is a deluge of new ideas with few other interactions being offered. As a class, we discuss what a more robust conversation looks and sounds like and why more types of interaction are necessary. Then we begin to practice building these pieces back into our interactions.

One strategy is to take a step back and remove their voices—and by this, I don't mean going back into the *Sh* zone. I mean literally ask them to talk without speaking—a silent discussion. In an analog model, the teacher writes a question in the center of a large sheet of paper or newsprint. After placing this question on a table, 4–5 students are each given a marker or crayon in a different color and are stationed in a circle around the table. The teacher sets a timer and tells them to begin responding the question. They draw lines from the question to their answer and then respond to their peers' thoughts by drawing lines from their writing to new bubbles. This continues until the time is up.

At the end of the discussion, have students reflect on their silent discussion—is there a prevalence of one color of writing on the page than another? Code the contributions as above and look for the variance of interactions. By having students discuss in this way, it equalizes each students' ability to participate to the conversation. No matter how prolific or quiet they may be in an oral conversation, they have equal access to the page. Of course, some limitations in terms of writing ability and language proficiency may present obstacles, in which case, considerations of appropriate accommodations or modifications should be given.

This method can also happen digitally, either in place of or subsequently following this activity. Private discussion boards are often tools in learning management systems (LMSs). You want to find one that allows for threaded replies (direct responses attached to the originating comment).

Once your students have practiced conversing in writing, try bringing their conversations out loud once again. At first, you may want to continue to monitor and code student interactions until you're confident that students have internalized this practice. Class Dojo fits this need. In addition to being a tool for class management, it can also be used to reinforce positive academic behaviors such as responding to a peer's question, using evidence in your example during a discussion, and so on.

STEP 3: TEACHER-MODERATED SHARING—DIPPING A TOE INTO SOCIAL MEDIA

After your students are fluent in collaborative discussion techniques, they are ready to take the show on the road. However, some teachers may want to give them practice sharing their voice with a wider audience than their own classmates. Students need to consider that their discussion group now consists of the whole world—and with this comes a myriad of points of view that they may not be familiar with. How might their ideas, statements, and opinions be perceived by others with different perspectives? Are they confident in their message? Do they feel ready to stand behind their statements?

Try practicing by engaging students in simulated Twitter chats. Provide questions or prompts and ask them to tweet their response using a simulated Twitter tool. I began this practice in my classroom by having a Twitter Tuesday each week and asking kids to share their thinking and respond to others in 140 characters or less. Colleagues took this idea and ran with it the following year, making it a schoolwide event each week and bringing all classes (K–8) into the fold.

As students share their thinking, teachers can give feedback on the messages and ultimately share these messages on social media on behalf of the student. Many teachers have one Twitter or Instagram account for the entire class and send out student messages, tagging them simply with initials or an avatar name. This allows kids to practice sharing safely and with guided feedback.

There are various tools you can use to simulate social media forums and scaffold student interaction with the wider world. Today's Meet is a closed discussion board that, like Twitter, limits kids to 140 characters. LMS discussion boards can also be used as a testing ground. Google forms can be used to submit test tweets. Websites such as GroupTweet allow for moderated tweeting.

Twitter Tuesday is something I had tried solo in my classroom back in 2011. On Tuesdays, I would have my students fill out a Google form with their reactions to our learning and questions they might have for experts around the world. After school, I would tweet their thoughts. While the students enjoyed this and many folks responded to their tweets, it didn't have the powerful impact I had hoped it would.

Two years later, two colleagues—Jenny Lynch and Jamila "Mia" Leonard—attended a PLAYDATE (see Chapter 14) and reinvented this idea for themselves. They envisioned Twitter Tuesday as a schoolwide sharing of ideas and learning. Each week, they would give their students a prompt and each class would respond. The teacher would tweet out these responses throughout the day under a shared Twitter handle—in this case, #ntalearns. Students from other classes would read and respond to tweets. Family and community members would engage and see what their children were learning. And yes, experts would share information and inspiration.

The result was incredible. From increased student engagement to even a guest Skype by author Mercer Mayer, here was the tangible impact not felt when my classroom had tweeted in isolation.

This idea has spread far and wide beyond Jenny's and Mia's classrooms. More schools around our network are adopting the concept and making it their own. Here are a few tips on how to get started with Twitter Tuesday in your school!

1. Create a short and easy-to-remember school hashtag. Make sure that it's as few characters as possible. Remember, you only have 140 characters including punctuation and spaces. The longer your hashtag, the less space you have for your student messages.

2. Research your hashtag before committing to it. Some of our schools hoped to have hashtags that were simply their school name and "rocks" or their school mascot. Remember that hashtags aren't proprietary. Anyone can use them. While you can't stop others from using your hashtag, you can try to use a hashtag that no one else is currently using. It's a bit confusing (and perhaps inappropriate) when student families log on to follow your school learning to find tweets about concerts, drinking, or other not-so-school-friendly topics.

3. Help each teacher to create a classroom Twitter handle. Just like a hashtag, classroom Twitter handles should be succinct (economy of characters) and school appropriate. Think classroom numbers, subjects, or mascots.

4. Create anchor charts to help students learn Twitter jargon. Jenny Lynch created a helpful visual for her students to learn about hashtags, retweets, and handles—all

confusing stuff for adults, much less six-year-olds! However, her display helped her students ease into this new world with confidence.

5. The teacher is the Tweeter. While the students create the ideas, the teacher is the one who tweets from the account. Children under the age of 13 can't use Twitter, according to its terms of service. To observe this rule, our teachers curate ideas from students either by having them share ideas in the classroom or submit ideas in Today's Meet. (Note: This tool is especially useful as it acts similar to a Twitter stream and limits them to 140 characters.) The teacher then tweets out ideas using the students' initials only.

STEP 4: OPENING THE GARDEN WALLS—DIVING INTO SOCIAL MEDIA

Once students have gained enough experience and practice strategies to be successful, the next step is to let them out into open water. Remember that they must be over 13 years old and must have parent permission. Also check with district rules and regulations around social media. However, if all lights are green, then the best thing you can do is provide ongoing support and guidance on how to craft a positive digital footprint and image. Many schools employ community-wide hashtags to steer student social media use toward the productive and positive.

East Leyden High School—just outside of Chicago, Illinois—is a fantastic example of this. The principal, Jason Markey, while working with two students and the school's activities director, began the schoolwide hashtag #leydenpride and a Twitter account for the school. He encouraged his high schoolers to tweet about their learning, successes, questions, school-related events, and so on using this hashtag. Eventually, he began turning the Twitter account itself to the kids as well. Each week, a different student would take the helm, attending school events and sharing his or her story to the world.

When I first heard of this, I asked Jason, "Don't kids abuse this? Don't disgruntled students write inappropriate comments on the hashtag?" His response was powerful. He explained that because the school empowered their student community with this hashtag and guided the positive and responsible use of it for promoting *pride* in their school, the students were the most tenacious guardians of its use. Rarely do negative messages pop up on the hashtag, but in the few cases when it has happened, it's the students who catch it first and respond most vehemently. Of course, the school responds as well, but since the culture and community are so strong, the students' response is the most powerful deterrent.

This is what we hope for as our students grow to inherit an increasingly digital world—not only the mindset and strategies to use technology in positive ways but also the ability to be upstanders in defending this space so it can continue to be used for good.

Now that your students have learned to harness the power of their voices, it's time to combine this with their cultivated curiosity, resilience, and productive playtime to use these powers for good. In the next chapter, we'll explore how to create learning experiences that are impactful not only for your students but also, possibly, for the world.

chapter 12

WITH GREAT POWER COMES GREAT RESPONSIBILITY

Once your students have begun to embrace wonder, solve problems, and share their voices, you've unlocked their power to create, share, and influence the world around them. However, as Spiderman's wise Uncle Ben said, "With great power comes great responsibility." As such, we need to make sure that our students are outfitted with the knowledge and skills to use these new abilities with respect and responsibility.

As their copilot in this edventure, your next step is to show them how to use their powers for good. Embolden your students to use their newfound empowerment to not simply be passive receivers and synthesizers of knowledge but to create and contribute to their community for the greater benefit of many. This is about taking the student agency you've built and leveraging it to help your class become change agents. In this chapter, we'll delve into how to help your students respond to real-world problems and share the narrative of their work.

REVISITING PROBLEM-BASED LEARNING

In Chapter 2, I briefly described problem-based learning (PBL; see Figure 12.1). As a refresher, PBL is an instructional approach where student learning

---

FIGURE 12.1 Problem-Based Learning

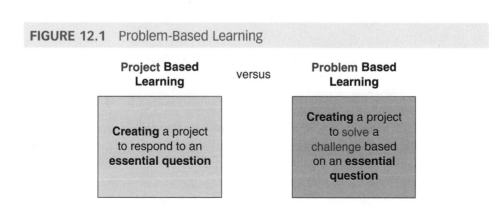

is centered around investigating and responding to an essential question (EQ) or challenge. Usually, this occurs over several weeks or longer (what is traditionally considered a *unit*) and involves cross-subject integration. At its highest level, the EQ is based in an authentic problem within students' everyday lives, and the ultimate goal is to build a response or solution to this problem. At the conclusion of the study, students showcase their learning and solution to an audience to disseminate their solution and to receive feedback.

Some people use the terms *problem-based learning* and *project-based learning* interchangeably. I would venture that they are slightly different. In my mind, **project**-based learning is when students create a project to respond to an EQ. The question may be derived from a real-world problem, but the project may be creating a public service announcement to educate people about it or a performance to analyze or synthesize the information. **Problem**-based learning is taking it a step further to first identify a **challenge** to respond to the question and then **solving** the challenge. It's about real action and taking that step from owning agency to becoming change agent.

This is a way to engage students in meaningful learning. It's the mindset of no longer asking students, "What do you want to be when you grow up?" but rather "Who do you want to be today?" In this way, we are no longer asking students to wait to matter. By asking students, "What do you want to be when you grow up?" we leave them in a state of waiting until the indeterminate future of "grown up" to utilize the skills we are giving them. Inherently, this kills a lot of motivation to grow and learn because "grown up" seems like an eternity away. Their current learning applies to a tomorrow they can't yet envision and don't yet care about. By asking them, "Who do you want to be today?" we are telling them, "You matter now. You can make a difference now." We are giving them the motivation to seek out new knowledge and make meaning of their world because the things they learn will affect and improve their here and now. Problem-based learning poses this question to our students where project-based learning doesn't necessarily do so. To avoid confusion throughout the rest of this chapter, any time I use the acronym *PBL*, I am referring to this deeper, more focused **problem**-based learning.

DIGGING IN TO PROBLEM-BASED LEARNING

Once you take your class through the steps in the previous two chapters, then they should be ready for this challenge. If you skipped to this section, you may want to backtrack to Chapter 10 to prepare your students. This kind of thinking and exploration requires students to have already internalized a level of curiosity, a clarity of purpose, and resilience in problem solving. If your kids already embrace these skills, then let's go!

Step 1: Finding the Problem-Based Essential Question

First off, you must identify an EQ or challenge. This can come from the questioning process outlined in Chapter 10 or from another source. What's important is that the question or challenge *comes from your students*. You can certainly prompt them with media, articles, or ideas, but let them come to the curiosity themselves. This is the focal point for the entire learning journey, so they must have intrinsic buy-in.

Resist the urge to give them multiple-choice options for problems to choose from. This limits the authenticity of the problem and thus the learning. They should identify the problem themselves because it's one that they perceive as affecting them or those around them. Don't worry about the problem seeming too monolithic or advanced for your students to solve. If they ask the question "Why can't scientists cure cancer?" the intention is not that they cure cancer themselves. It's that they familiarize themselves with the problem and come up with a challenge for someone to respond to. For example, they might build a public health program to educate their community about low-cost cancer care options.

Although you don't want to limit their exploration of problems, you can certainly give them guidelines and guidance for selecting a problem. If they come to you with *Questdones,* or questions with finite answers (see Chapter 10 for more information), push them to think bigger and aim higher. I like to share the quote from Astro Teller with my students: "Our ambitions are a glass ceiling to what we can accomplish." I also like to show inspirational videos of others students accomplishing great things. Visit the companion website for a current playlist of sample videos (see QR Code 12).

QR Code 12

In addition to serving them inspiration and taking them through a curiosity/questioning process, you can also help them understand how to pose the problem in the form of a powerful EQ from which they may build their PBL challenge.

An EQ must be

- without a "correct" answer,
- worth deeper exploration or understanding, and
- born from student curiosity.

Examples of EQs include the following:

- Why aren't there more female engineers?
- Why are people in my community afraid of the police?
- Why aren't there better grocery stores or healthier restaurants in my neighborhood?
- How can we make dismissal safer?

Step 2: Developing the Challenge

Once your students have determined an EQ, they should begin to research the question to understand it and learn more about the problem. Before they can determine a challenge to respond to the problem, they first must understand it. Allow them to do web research, utilize the resources in your library, interview community members and classmates, and even send out surveys to a wider audience if that's appropriate. Give them time to collect, synthesize, and make meaning of this research with the greater goal of finding a challenge to respond to or even solving this question.

Sometimes the question may even evolve as the students become more involved in their research; they may realize they didn't ask the right question or perhaps they find another pathway that seems more interesting. This is completely fine and even encouraged. Remember, we *want* them to follow that breadcrumb trail of wonder. This is about allowing your students to lead the way.

Once your kids have gotten more familiar with the question, it's time to craft the challenge itself. The challenge isn't an answer to the question, as any good EQ is inherently unanswerable. And yet it should *respond* to the question. See the table below for some examples.

Examples of Creating Challenges for Essential Questions

ESSENTIAL QUESTION	CHALLENGE
Why aren't there more female engineers?	Create a girls-in-engineering club at school
Why are people in my community afraid of the police?	Develop a program in which local police volunteer in schools
Why aren't there better grocery stores or healthier restaurants in my neighborhood?	Create a social media campaign to bring healthier food options to our community
How can we make dismissal safer?	Organize a student-led dismissal patrol program

Note that the challenges are programs or initiatives that don't necessarily give a direct answer to the problem posed in the question but instead show initiative to alleviate or educate others on that problem. Building a challenge can be the trickiest part. Whereas when determining the problem, you didn't want to limit students with words like *too big* or *impossible*, when developing a challenge, students should take inventory of their resources:

- What physical resources do you need to meet this challenge?
- Do you have any funding? If not, can you fundraise?
- What support from adults will you require, if any?
- How much time will this take?
- Do you have to learn any new skills to complete this challenge?

Step 3: Rising to the Challenge

Before beginning to attack the challenge, your students will want to build out a self-assessment framework to measure success. If you're looking to grade this work, this is a great place to start (more on assessment in a bit). Work with your students to help them answer questions like the following:

- How will I know when this challenge is successfully completed?
- If it fails, how will I measure my efforts?
- What is the timeline within which I expect to complete this challenge?

What follows is purposeful playtime. It's time for your students to tinker, create plans, and iterate on them to complete their challenge. Each day, they should begin by refocusing on the EQ, share any newfound knowledge or information about it, and revisit their challenge. As they invent and explore, they may determine that they need to pivot the focus of their challenge or reevaluate their knowledge of the EQ. This is totally fine. It's the process of exploration, creation, and empowerment that is key.

From the very beginning of this process, your students should be reflecting daily, if not more. As I emphasized in previous chapters, reflection on all levels is vital. As you release more and more control to your students and turn the ship over to them, you must help them stop to check their course frequently. An easy and powerful way to do this is to have your students create a blog to capture their progress. Give them a list of questions to ponder as they write their posts each day (see Figure 12.2). Take the self-assessment guidelines they created at the beginning of the PBL process and add them to these reflection questions for each day. How are they progressing according to their own standards? What pivots or course changes will they need to make tomorrow if they're no longer headed in the right direction? What failures did they encounter, and what did they learn from these failures (i.e., what will they do differently in the future)? Encourage your students to capture lots of video, images, notes, doodles, and ideas and upload them to their blog as they go. I like to show them archives of scientists' journals as a model for this.

These blogs are also a great way to provide grades if they are something your school is requiring for this unit. Rather than grading whether their PBL challenge is successful—which it may not be—you're grading their learning process. The challenge is simply an effect of the overall experience.

The blog can be more structured. You can create a rubric for what must be included in each post and even questions they must respond to. I usually call these *reflection guides* and require that students answer a certain number of questions from this guide in each post.

FIGURE 12.2 Reflection Guide

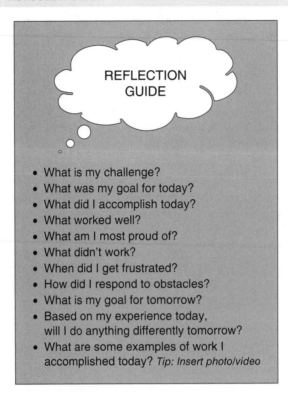

Step 4: Showcasing the Learning

Once your students have completed their challenges, it's time to share. This can be done in the form of a showcase, website, or a film festival. Whether it's a face-to-face event or a virtual exhibition, they should have a chance to share their challenge and solution with their community and receive feedback. This allows them to validate their efforts and get ideas for the future.

Have your students also share the guidelines they created for themselves to measure their own success. In their presentations, ask them to do some self-reflection in front of the audience. They can even use pictures, videos, and attachments from their blog posts to illustrate their journey and enrich their showcase.

THE ROLE OF THE TEACHER

What do you do as the teacher? Aside from playing facilitator to support their questioning and to help them in selecting a challenge and reflecting daily, you also help them fill in the gaps in their knowledge required to complete the challenge. As students are working, they should begin to identify the skills and competencies they lack but require to be successful. In some cases, they'll need you to help them see these needs. This is where you get to teach!

Create mini lessons to fill in their knowledge gaps and aid in their exploration. It was amazing to me how in the same year I tried to teach a traditional algebra unit to no avail, but months later, when my students were attempting to write a grant as part of a PBL challenge and needed to balance a budget, all of the sudden, algebra became the most interesting topic in the world. I had some of my most math-phobic students clamoring over Xs and Ys and hungering over a balanced equation. Build time into the unstructured periods of PBL for the students to meet with you for skill building in addition to routine reflection and progress check-ins.

If you're looking for more information on PBL, check out the book *The 20Time Project* by Kevin Brookhouser.

PROBLEM-BASED LEARNING SPOTLIGHT— KIDTREK: A SAFE JOURNEY APP FOR STUDENTS

One of my first forays into PBL was supporting my students as they investigated the EQ, "How can we make it safer for students to get around our neighborhood?" My students shared that they often felt uncomfortable walking home due to certain individuals in their community and the constant traffic coming from the two highway exits near our school. They wanted to find a way to help students get home safely and quickly. After creating some student surveys and interviewing police, community members, and school staff, they determined that the challenge they wanted to pursue was creating an app to address these concerns. They found an app design contest and built their challenge around this opportunity. Within a month, they had designed a new app concept called KidTREK. Below is an excerpt from their proposal as well as their pitch video (see the QR code). While they ultimately didn't win the contest, they brought awareness to the issues and helped inform their peers on ways to be smarter and safer during their travels to and from school.

···· KidTREK: A Safe Journey App for Kids ····

Ever walked home and felt nervous that someone was going to hurt you in some kind of way? Ever met someone that was hurt on their way home? Ever worried about whether your child, student or relative was getting to their destination safely? Well we have an app for you! This app is called KidTREK. This app will let your parent, family member, friend, guardian, teacher or principal track you while you're on your way home, after sports, clubs, etc. This is a great app to protect your kids and make sure they're safe.

goo.gl/h3qJV3

(Continued)

(Continued)

We are concerned about the safety of children as they travel from location to location. As middle school students in Chicago, we are coming to and from school on our own every day. We also have to go to our friends' houses, family's houses and activities by ourselves. A lot of times we feel nervous. Our parents, teachers, friends and family members are always worried about us too. They call us to make sure we're safe. We worry about whether we can call 911 fast enough if someone comes to bother us. We worry about bullies trying to bother us. We want an app that helps the people who care about us track where we are and see if we are safe.

If you register KidTREK with a parent, guardian, or school you will be able to track your child or student when they leave from where they are coming from and when they arrive home or where they are going. You will get a text when your child leaves their location with a link to their changing location and another text when they arrive at their destination. This text feature uses GPS Tracking. Another feature we have is when a school or a parent wants to track that child at any time, they have the ability to do that. If they feel like that child is in danger they can track them. It will also have automated tips about crossing the street. This means the app will use GPS to know when a child gets close to a crosswalk so it can give automated safety tips. For example when you are approaching a sidewalk it reminds you to look both ways which could be helpful (could be turned off). This app can tell you where police stations are and when you are near one (can be turned off). We are also excited to let you know that our app has a program that will invite neighborhood businesses apply to become KidTREK certified Safe Havens. This will allow kids to go into this place if they feel like they are being followed or are in danger. The business will call 911 or their parent. To identify these locations, the windows will have a certified sticker.

THE STUDENT BECOMES THE MASTER

As students have more experiences where they are identifying challenges and creating positive change in their community, they will have more stories to share. Beyond the showcase aspect of PBL, it's helpful for you as their copilot in this adventure to help them spread their story. They can do this in a myriad of ways. I have repeated the power of blogs and social media throughout this text, but you may also consider bringing your students to share in person as well.

Teacher conferences are a great place to learn and grow as an educator. However, too often, we gather as educators to talk about what's best for kids without bringing any actual kids to the table. By inviting in students to hear and share the learning at this event, you create a level of authenticity and honesty throughout the day. Additionally, in giving them the stage, you allow them the opportunity to have a hand in shaping their own education system.

FIGURE 12.3 Students at Teacher Learning Event

I began bringing my students to present at conferences when we began our Power to the Pupil adventure. Colleagues near and far leaned in to hear how the students felt about their learning experiences, what was important to them, and what they hoped to change. I've seen students of all ages (K–12) step up to the mic and steal the show at teacher learning events, from informal staff meetings to large-scale conferences (see Figure 12.3). While these sessions are not only incredibly engaging, it is also so powerful to hear from a student why a specific pedagogy works.

If your students aren't ready to lead an entire session on their own, consider App Speed Dating. This is a concept I first experienced in Auburn, Maine, as part of their Leveraging Learning Conference. At this event, kindergarteners led groups of teachers through quick, hands-on app workshops. After seeing this, I brought the idea back to Chicago and have used the concept many times to support both teachers and students in learning new concepts, apps, and ideas in a fun, constructive way.

Each student sits at a table with 5–6 devices, all preloaded with their app, program, or idea (see Figure 12.4). As participants come into the room, they get a number and sit at their designated table. When the first buzzer goes off, the students have 3–5 minutes (depending on the total session time) to help the participants explore the app and learn how they use it in class. When the buzzer rings again, participants move on to the next station. My colleague Kristin Ziemke (@kristinziemke) pushed this idea up a notch by giving her first graders business cards to hand out at the end of the session! We've used this idea as well, giving our kids cards with a QR code that links to their blog or classroom Twitter handle.

Another idea is having your students live-report the event when they aren't busy presenting. This is another idea hailing from Auburn, Maine's Leveraging Learning Conference. Tech Coordinator Carl Bucciantini supported his

FIGURE 12.4 App Speed Dating

middle schoolers as they live-tweeted the entire event from various school Twitter accounts. Two students went to each session and used Today's Meet as a back channel to preview tweets with their peer editors (who sat in a central room, moderating tweets for consistency, grammar, and message). Once the peer editor approved the tweet, the student posted it on Twitter. As a result, not only could any educator in the world follow the amazing learning and ideas from the event but the students also brought a higher level of authenticity to the professional learning.

Now that you've handed over the wheel to your students, empowered them with the ability and confidence to steer their ship to exciting new learning destinations, and kept them on track with regular reflection times, what's left for you to do? How do you know if your path stayed true and you truly reached your intended destination? Have you truly discovered Innovation Island? In Part IV of this book, we will take a moment to evaluate your practice and learn how to stay inspired beyond this journey.

part IV

REFLECTING ON YOUR EDVENTURE

The most courageous act is still to think for yourself. Aloud.

—Coco Chanel

chapter 13

EVALUATING YOUR PRACTICE

As you work through your Teacher Innovation Exploration Plan, FAIL[1] forward and iterate to SAIL[2], and push into deeper waters to explore the seas of student agency, you will need a way to reflect and evaluate your progress. Are you still on a course toward elusive Innovation Island? Are things truly different and better as a result of your technology use? There are many models to guide this reflection. In this chapter, we will explore a few and consider how to use them to keep you SAILing in the right direction (pun intended).

LOOPING IN YOUR CRITICAL FRIEND

In Chapter 2, I suggested finding a Critical Friend to help you stay on course during this journey. Hopefully you've already recruited someone, and if not, perhaps you have someone in mind. In any case, your Critical Friend should also be looped into whatever framework or reflection tool you're using to measure your progress. As you read through the different models below, bring your Critical Friend into the discussion and make sure he or she has the same language and understanding before you set off on your innovation exploration.

REVISITING THE SAMR AND TIM FRAMEWORKS

In Chapter 1, we explored the SAMR (substitution, augmentation, modification, redefinition) and TIM (Technology Integration Matrix) frameworks (refer to Chapter 1 for a more detailed review of both models). In self-reflection, I like beginning with SAMR as it's simpler to use and has a clear linear flow. There are many ways to use this model, but consider using it as a quick calibration tool for your planning and reflection.

---

[1]First Attempt In Learning; see Chapter 5 on embracing failure.

[2]Subsequent Attempt In Learning; see Chapter 5 on embracing failure.

As I sketched out student activities, I would reference the SAMR model to ask myself, "Is the technology making this better?" I would compare the analog version of the activity to the digitized update. I would then try and place it on the scale. Remember, as with any framework, the SAMR model can be objective. It's not about finding the exact accurate measure of the learning activity on the continuum but the process of reflection and questioning that's important.

After my students completed the activity, I would revisit the framework to see if I still agreed with its placement on the scale. As I continued in my practice, I was able to use this method as a compass to keep me on that trajectory toward different and better. Below are some questions to ask yourself to push from one level of the SAMR model to the next.

LEVELING UP WITH THE SAMR MODEL

First, identify the activity you are reflecting upon and the goal the activity is designed to meet. Then, once you've identified the SAMR level of the activity, ask yourself the following questions:

LEVEL	QUESTIONS
Substitution to Augmentation	• What could I improve in this activity? • How can technology help me improve it? • Can I get the same thing done with paper and pencil? If so, why am I using the technology? • What tools are out there that could provide more opportunities for my students? • Is there way I could do this (faster, more often, better, smarter, more effectively)?
Augmentation to Modification	• Is this the right task to meet the goal? • If I were to redesign the task to better meet the goal, what would it look like? • What are the barriers to completing the goal? • Why did I decide to use technology in the first place? • Did I meet the need originally motivating me to introduce technology?
Modification to Redefinition	• If I had a magic wand, how would I want this goal to be met? • How can I elevate this goal to the next level? • What autonomy or agency can I give to my students in completing this goal through technology? • How can I use technology to not only address this goal but others simultaneously?

Once I had a handle of where I was going, I would use the TIM to make more finite course adjustments. If I felt things were already going well, this model would allow me to refine my practice even further so as to better focus on the strategies I was trying out with my students. Because the TIM is so heavily immersed in classroom teacher language and so focused on learning tools, it helps the teacher who is already somewhat familiar with what good technology use looks like but wants to take the next step to improve his or her practice. Consider the following flow for using the TIM to reflect on your journey.

APPROACHING THE THREE DIMENSIONS OF THE TIM

1. First look at what the students are doing. How do they measure up in the student dimension of the TIM? What level of technology integration and what characteristics of a healthy learning environment are evident in your classroom?

2. Next, outline steps to move to higher levels of student agency in the TIM.

3. If you're ready to take it from two dimensions, see how your teacher practice impacts student learning by measuring yourself in the teacher dimension of the TIM.

4. Based on your self-assessment in the framework, outline what steps can you take that support the action plan to increase student agency that you've already outlined.

5. After you've taken a stab at evaluating your students and yourself, dig into the classroom setting dimension. This one can either be the easiest or the most difficult to approach. Either teachers use this as the first step and spend weeks rearranging materials and furniture without changing their practice or they don't have the power to change their classroom set up and get stymied. In any case, begin with students, then yourself, and save this one for last.

SHARING YOUR ADVENTURE

Sometimes the best way to get support is to share. When I first began my innovation quest, I spent a lot of time talking to my Critical Friends and reading blogs. One day, my friend and mentor, Carrie Kamm, suggested I begin writing my own blog. I immediately began to laugh. Who has time to blog? I was busy redefining my practice, failing forward, and trying my best not to drown in all of the other daily duties that come with the exciting life of a teacher. But Carrie was insistent. She told me that writing down my experiences is excellent reflection and doing so publicly will allow me to get more authentic and frequent feedback.

I was terrified. My fears were vast in magnitude and number: What if I had nothing to say? I don't know what I'm doing yet! What if no one reads my blog? What if people *do* read my blog and then judge me? When would I find the time?

Well, first off, I had *plenty* to say. Every day was an adventure in trial and error and I talked off the ear of anyone who would listen to me. (In retrospect, maybe Carrie was telling me to blog so I'd stop loitering in her office every afternoon.)

Second, if no one reads the blog, then the exercise in writing down my thoughts would still be cathartic. As mentioned in an earlier chapter, a blog that no one reads is just a diary.

Third, if people did read the blog, I had to get over the fear of being judged. I was being brave enough to try something new. I also had to be brave enough to share what I was trying. If I was honest about my attempts and earnest in my reflection, that would have to be enough for those who may see my words.

Finally, there was the time aspect. As I continued my experiments in changing my practice, I realized that this was a big investment for me, both emotionally and in time. If I was going to spend that much time researching and iterating, taking time to reflect should be just as important.

So I took the plunge. I began my blog on Wednesday, March 30, 2011, before I went to school. I hit "Post" and ran out the door to catch the train for work (see Figure 13.1). I had no idea whether anyone would read it and if they did, what they would think.

By the end of the day, I had four comments. Granted, they were all people I knew, but they were affirmation of this reflection process. One comment that really struck me was from my friend Bruce:

> One thing busy educators don't do for themselves is provide some time to pause and reflect. Pause, and think about the path you have traveled, and where you would like to go, rather than floating like a chip on the lake. Savor your experiences, the easy ones and the hard ones, both contribute to growth. So thanks so much for the place to pause, and contributing to our techie using teacher community.

Five years, 182 posts, 642 comments, and 1.5 million page views later, I have not received a single mean-hearted message. Sure, there were some constructive criticisms, but that's why I began this blog: to share my adventure, get feedback, and help me grow. I have gained collaborative relationships with fellow educators and learned more about my own practice through blogging.

So consider beginning your blog, *especially* now that you're at the beginning of your journey. This is when you have the most to say and when you will be growing the most. Are you a coach or administrator who supports classroom teachers? You should be blogging, too! Share your ideas, your inspiration, and what drives you. We are teaching our students to share, cultivate their voices, and think out loud. We should be modeling this in our own practice.

FIGURE 13.1 Teaching Like It's 2999

WEDNESDAY MARCH 30, 2011

Well here I am

I've been encouraged by colleagues to start a blog (to write about my exploration of technology in the classroom). However I kept thinking: a) I have no time to blog, b) What if people think what I'm saying is crazy/'stupid' c) Who would even want to read this?

Well I guess we'll see... so here goes nothing:

****

First off, let me tell you a little about myself. I am currently a 5th grade math, science and writing teacher in an urban school district -- teaching at a PK-8 school with a student body that is predominantly high needs and African American. I have been teaching here for 6 years and have loved each one - thanks to my kids. I feel like this school is my family now and don't know how I could ever leave. After 'growing up' as an educator with this school, teaching in the same 4-5th grade band for several years, I was beginning to feel like I was hitting my stride. I thought, OK -- I got this. Then, my world was completely changed thanks to a grant approval for 32 iPads.

When I heard that the grant had won, I cried. My husband said, "Ohhh... how sweet! You're so happy!" I replied, "Nooooo! I'm crying because I'm scared now... I have to actually do all those things I said I'd do in that grant!" Oh dear...

Although daunting, I took on the challenge with a deep breath and willingness to try, fail and try again. I received the iPads in August of 2010. Since that time we've been working to integrate them into our daily instruction. So far we've been fairly successful. If you were to walk into my classroom on any given day, you will see them out and being used throughout each subject - math, science, writing... even a little social science for good measure. These shiny little devices have single handedly transformed my differentiation, assessment and outlook on what can be done in the classroom. On a daily basis, I think wow -- is this really happening?

We've received much positive feedback from parents, colleagues, administration, district personnel and even the kind folks at Apple. Yet the questions I keep asking myself are - how effectively are we using them? What could we do better? How can I push both myself and my students to use this technology more efficiently, effectively? In this blog, I'll be exploring the ups and downs, ins and outs of answering these questions....

Posted by Jennie Magiera ✉ ✏

M ▣ ▸ f ⓟ G+1 Recommend this on Google

Here are some tips for starting your blog:

- **Pick a platform**. There are lots of blogging sites to use, but two popular ones are Google's Blogger and WordPress. They are both free, so try them both on for size. See which one is easier for you, the devices you prefer, and your style. Test drive them before you go live, as once you pick a platform, it's best to stick with it.

- **Don't be shy about writing your first "Hello, world" post.** This is often the most difficult post to write. It's introducing you, your voice, and your ideas to the world for the first time. I wrote mine as if I were writing an e-mail to my best friends. That tends to get the most genuine version of your voice out easily and quickly. In the first draft, don't worry about grammar, spelling, and content. Just get it out. Then go back and edit with various audiences in mind. Would you be okay with your principal seeing this? Your superintendent? Your colleagues? The parents of your students? Your parents? If not, consider revising.
- **Make a list of potential blog topics.** If you were like me, you secretly have a load of things about which you have opinions. If so, write them down in a list and use these as fodder for future posts. If not, then treat your blog as a daily journal. What's happening in your classroom today? What worked? What didn't work? Use the world as your personal reflection. However, each time you post, remember to revise with the audience in mind. Unless you restrict your blog to certain viewers (which I don't recommend—it limits your access to support and a diversity of ideas) then you want to keep in mind that anyone can see your words.
- **Practice good digital citizenship.** Just as we teach our students to protect their digital identity, so should you. Safeguard what you share about the location of your school, names of students, images of student work, and images of the kids themselves. Even if you're writing about work you're doing with a colleague, be careful about including media or names that identify your colleagues. If you think that including more specific info or media containing faces or work would be helpful for your post, be sure to get permission from students, their families, and/or your colleagues first.

TAKING IT A STEP FURTHER: PRESENTING YOUR STORY

For some people, public speaking is scarier than a room full of snakes. However, once you start sharing your story virtually, it can be nice to do the same in front of a live audience. The questions and connections that result are often even more powerful than those you make online. Additionally, many educational conferences offer waived or reduced registration fees if you give a presentation. For a teacher with limited funds, this may allow you to squeeze in that learning opportunity that you otherwise couldn't afford.

When submitting a proposal for a presentation, here are some suggestions to help you increase your chances of being accepted:

- **Use your blog!** If you've taken my advice and begun blogging, your posts are ripe with ideas for powerful presentations. Find one that you are especially passionate about and summarize it into a presentation.

- **A picture tells a thousand words.** No one likes sitting in a presentation that's a parade of text-heavy slides. Try and use images from your classroom, examples of student work, and media that your kids have created. Your greatest strength is your experience as an educator, so let that shine. If you do have to include text in a slide, try to keep it both big and small. By this I mean, use large and clear font (over 30 pt.) and keep your word count as low as possible (less than 10 words).
- **Create a catchy title.** People say "don't judge a book by its cover," but let's be honest . . . many of us do. Similarly, conference attendees and submission reviewers judge a session by its title. You want one that is clear but also catchy. For example, if you're presenting about using Google Forms for assessment, avoid a didactic title such as *Google Forms for Student Assessment* or something unclear like *Clicking Our Way to Success!* Instead combine the two to find a balance: *A New Form of Assessment: Google Forms for Student Assessment.*
- **Brush up on your presentation skills.** Watch a few TED talks (http://www.ted.com) and you'll see that the presenters seem comfortable, natural. They are telling stories and sharing their passion with the audience, not reading a book report. You'll want to have the same presence when you share your classroom stories. There is a great book called *Weekend Language: Presenting With More Stories and Less PowerPoint* by Andy Craig and Dave Yewman. It is chock-full of tips on not only how to present at conferences but how to communicate more clearly and effectively. I highly recommend it!

Hopefully this chapter gave you some ideas to begin reflecting on both in the privacy of your own classroom and out loud for all to see (and read). In the next chapter, I will share some ideas for how to continue your learning and get more support. There, you will find lists of conferences that you may want to attend—or perhaps submit a proposal to present at!

chapter 14

STAYING INSPIRED AND FINDING SUPPORT

N ow that you've had your edventure, how can you find support and fresh ideas? If you're still on the journey, how do you stay inspired to keep going when it's not smooth sailing? As Ellen Potter once said, "All great adventures have moments that are really crap." You'll need a way to keep going through that . . . crap. In this chapter, we will explore powerful places to find that inspiration.

CREATING A PROFESSIONAL LEARNING NETWORK THAT WORKS

When taking on an endeavor like transforming your practice, being part of a community helps motivate you, feeds your passion, and provides support during those FAIL (First Attempt In Learning) moments (see Chapter 5 for more information about embracing failure). A PLN can take many different shapes, but here are a few tips to consider when forming your network.

Professional Learning Communities and Professional Learning Networks

Some people use professional learning community (PLC) and professional learning network (PLN) interchangeably, but there are many arguments out there for why and how they are different. One suggested difference is that a PLC is a face-to-face group whereas a PLN is online. Another belief is that a PLC is more formalized, goal oriented, and school or district based whereas a PLN is formed more organically out of like-minded individuals.

To me, they work together. In my mind, a PLN is made up of many smaller, often connected, PLCs. For example, you might belong to a PLC formed around a specific affinity, such as device preference or grade level. You might also belong to another PLC formed around a common geography, school, or district. These various PLCs may interconnect in membership and ideals, but these communities come together to be your network. As such, your network can cross interest groups, geographies, and topics.

When building your PLN, consider the different PLCs you're a part of. How many of them are formal, how many are informal? Do you have growth areas or learning needs that aren't yet met by these communities? Consider local, state, or national groups you can join to push and promote your goals.

http://www.iste .org/lead/affiliate- directory

One place to start is your local International Society for Technology in Education (ISTE) affiliate. ISTE is a global "nonprofit organization serving educators and education leaders committed to empowering connected learners in a connected world" (see the adjacent QR code and http://www.iste.org/about for more information). Most states as well as many countries around the globe have an ISTE affiliate. These affiliates can help you begin building your PLN, as they contain many PLCs within each.

Cultivating Constructive Conflict

As you build your PLN, look for a range of ideas and perspectives. As most PLNs are made up of various affinity-based PLCs, it's easy to end up in an echo chamber. You throw out an idea and receive a chorus of "Yes, amazing!" and "Love it! +1!" or "Nailed it! You rock!" statements. While affirmation and support are reinforcements when tackling challenges, it's also good to have a bit of conflict—colleagues who will give you an unexplored perspective to consider.

When I build or join PLCs to be a part of my greater network, I look for individuals who will push my thinking and cause me to question my ideas. This isn't meant as a way to knock me down or discourage me but to sharpen and improve my approaches and philosophies to be more robust and well rounded.

A Shared Space

Once you have joined or created your PLCs and PLNs, it's important that you have a shared space to collaborate, ask questions, and share ideas. Here are some options for that space. This table offers both virtual and face-to-face options, but a mix of both is ideal. A truly powerful PLN has aspects of both: face-to-face meetings for play, conversation, and building relationships and virtual forums for those in-between times to continue the conversation.

SHARED SPACE	VIRTUAL/ FACE-TO-FACE	PROS	CONS
Twitter	Virtual	Good for quick information and a global audience	Difficult to track at times The pace may be too fast for some
Google+ or Facebook	Virtual	Community of learners already inhabit this space for personal sharing, so it is easy to get attention and frequent interaction Static page to see updates and replies to discussions	Not much customization on community pages Some may not like to mix personal social media use with professional use Some schools block these sites
Shared Blog	Virtual	Allows for learners to explore ideas and share information in a private space, which can be made public down the line Site available at all schools Easy to respond to posts	Some may be daunted by having to write a full blog post; a short Facebook post or Tweet may seem less intimidating
Customized Website or Learning Management System (LMS)	Virtual	LMS sites have built-in communities and there are other sites geared directly toward PLN collaboration Various tools are available to customize the platform to your needs	This is another place to login, so activity in this space may be sporadic
Video Chats: Google Hangouts/ Skype	Virtual	Allows for more personal face-to-face interaction and conversation	Requires scheduling a time when everyone is free
Scheduled Meet-Ups	Face-to-face	Allows for more organic face-to-face interaction Multiple conversations can be had at once Deeper connections made	Requires scheduling a time when everyone is free Requires everyone to be in same geographic area
Teacher-Led Unconferences	Face-to-face	Allows for more formal learning with an open schedule Deeper connections can be made	Requires planning Requires scheduling a time when everyone is free Requires everyone to be in same geographic area

TEACHER-LED LEARNING EVENTS

As you look for support and expand your PLN, you'll find that teacher-led learning events are the perfect fit for your needs. The content of these events is driven by the participants and therefore is usually more closely aligned to your needs.

If you're brave enough to speak up as an attendee, you can even directly impact the focus of your learning while you're there. Two of these "unconferences" (informal learning events) to consider are EdCamps and PLAYDATEs. The latter is a shameless plug, which you will see as you read on.

EdCamps

EdCamp is a model of unconference that originated in 2010 based on the BarCamp model. BarCamp has nothing to do with drinking; rather, it's an event structure that allows the participant to direct the learning options throughout the day. The team that organized the first EdCamp attended BarCamp Philly in 2009 and decided to create an education-focused version of this event—thus EdCamp was born.

EdCamps are usually one-day events that must be free and are learner driven. Participants arrive and crowdsource topics they want to share or discuss and rooms are assigned organically. The result is an ad-hoc schedule created on the spot by the participants. The rest of the day is spent ducking in and out of these sessions where participants are also the presenters. Depending on the crowd of attendees, the sessions vary in style from hands-on to discussion-based to a more formal presentation.

My favorite part about EdCamps is how egalitarian they are. Everyone is an equal—anyone can suggest an idea. This creates a tone of collegiality and friendliness amongst the crowd. If you choose to attend an EdCamp, be sure to chat up your neighbor in a session and be ready to share.

For more information on where you can find an EdCamp near you—or host your own—visit their site (http://www.edcamp.org/).

PLAYDATEs

PLAYDATE is another unconference model that I cocreated with a group of edufriends.[1] Three of us—myself, Autumn Laidler, and Sue Gorman—were on a plane coming back from an educational technology conference and chatting about what we'd learned. We all agreed that we valued meeting new educators and discussing the good gospel that is innovative technology use. And yet, we also lamented that we learn about a myriad of new tools, websites, tricks, and apps at these conferences only to go back to the real world and have little to no time (usually the latter) to ever master or even simply explore any of it. For me, they usually end up in my "to explore" task list.

---

[1] Autumn Laidler @MsLaider, Sue Gorman @sjgorman, Kristin Ziemke @kristinziemke, Carolyn Skibba @skibtech, Ben Kovacs @kovacsteach

Thus the idea of PLAYDATE was born. I originally wanted to call it "ExploriCON" but as the nature of Autumn's and my relationship goes, we ping-ponged ideas off each other until we got a shinier version of this original thought. First, Autumn came up with PLAY—People Learning and Asking "Y." Then Sue joined in the acronym fun and suggested adding DATE. Autumn found a perfect acronym for that—Digital Age Teacher Exploration. And so PLAYDATE came about. After coming up with the acronym (because as educators, we love acronyms), we refined the idea to meet some of our unaddressed professional learning needs and leverage best practices we'd seen at other conferences.

Once we landed, I stayed up late that night creating a website and registration form and beginning to throw our ideas on paper. We recruited three more friends into the fold: Ben Kovacs, Kristin Ziemke, and Carolyn Skibba. Together, we put on the first PLAYDATE three months later. Surprisingly, the word got out even before our event went live, and so the first PLAYDATE actually happened concurrently in three locations: Portland, Boston, and Chicago.

The PLAYDATE conference model is geared toward those who just want to explore—or play with—apps, websites, programs, or tools that they've always wanted to dig into more deeply but never had the time or support to do so. Modeled after an unconference or an EdCamp, the sessions are participant driven and hands on. These events call educators together to sit in a room for a few hours and just *play*. Most importantly, there is "no sit and get learning." No presenters. No slide decks. Period. All of the content is learner driven, exploration based, and hands-on, just like the model of education we hope to develop for our students. The PLAYDATE is simply time to tinker and explore.

The only structure is the timing of the day (usually 1- or 2-hour play blocks) and themed rooms based on strategies, ideas, tools, or challenges. For example, one room might be filled with Makey-Makey kits and allow teachers to fiddle around and build. Another may find educators huddled around screens trying to learn to code. And yet another room could be bustling with video production and editing. At the end, there is a sharing of learning and takeaways, cheekily dubbed "The Play Off," and digital content and notes from each "PlayRoom" are disseminated to all.

So far, there have been over 40 PLAYDATES across eight different countries. We have shared the PLAYDATE planning kit and information as an open source Google Drive folder with only three stipulations:

- It must be free.
- The event should be based around play and choice.
- There should not be any presenters or presentations.

The simplistic nature of a PLAYDATE makes it easy to host your own event or even do a mini-PLAYDATE after school in your classroom or during a staff meeting. I've seen many colleagues begin to take teacher-directed professional learning time to hold informal PLAYDATE sessions in their classrooms. They send out a message to their staff or team inviting them to meet up and play. And then they do! Just like that.

For more information on where you can find a PLAYDATE near you—or host your own—visit the site (http://bit.ly/playdateconference).

For Coaches and Administrators: Three-Date Model to EdTech Learning

For those readers who are providing support to teachers on this expedition (i.e., coaches, coordinators, and administrators), here is a more structured system of professional support to try out. As your teacher teams delve into their Teacher Innovation Exploration Plans (TIEPs), space out the following professional learning experiences in the following order:

Experience #1—App Speed Dating: Begin with a student-led session called App Speed Dating (see Chapter 12 for more information). Recruit students in your school to share their favorite apps, strategies, and programs. Ask them to practice teaching them to others, and make sure they can not only explain *how* to use the tool in their classroom but also *why* someone would want to use it.

Then have teachers come in for 60 to 90 minutes of rotational stations set up like, well . . . speed dating. Each teacher gets a dance card with two blank lines on one side and table number on the other side. That number corresponds to the student-led station at which they will begin. As the session commences, the student station leaders have a set amount of time (usually 5 minutes) to make their teachers fall in love with their selected strategy or tool. After the time has elapsed, a bell goes off and the teachers move to the next table for another round of exploration. This continues until all tables have been visited.

At the end of all of the speed-sharing sessions, the teachers can go back to two stations that piqued their interest. They select these stations by adding them to the blank lines on the back of their dance card. We call this "going back for a second dance." They can then spend a bit longer asking the student teacher follow-up questions.

Experience #2—PLAYDATE: After the App Speed Dating experience, teachers will most likely have a few ideas they want to try out. Give them the time and space to do this by hosting a small PLAYDATE. Allow them the time to tinker with what they discovered in App Speed Dating and explore how it might meet the needs in their TIEP.

Experience #3—The Third Date: Originally, this model only had two steps—App Speed Dating and PLAYDATE. However, an educator from Brisbane, Australia, by the name of Miriam Scott (@mskroker) reached out to me via Twitter to let me know I was forgetting an important phase: The Third Date (see Figure 14.1). She explained that in the first date,

FIGURE 14.1   Third Date Tweet

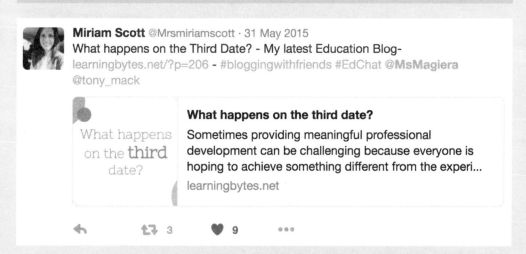

App Speed Dating, you meet the strategy or tool. In the second date, PLAYDATE, you get to know it a bit better and decide if you are a good fit. The Third Date is when you take it home (wink, wink). Even without the cheeky double meaning, Miriam has a point. While learning about new strategies and tools is a good thing and getting practice and experience with them even better, the real power comes in trying them out in your classroom. The Third Date is about applying this learning to your TIEP, reflecting on the process, and sharing your successes or attempts in learning.

There you have it: the Three Date model for professional learning. Feel free to rename it based on your community's culture and climate, but keep in mind the main tenants of this model: student voice, teacher choice, and play.

FORMAL LEARNING EVENTS

Finally, we can't forget about formal conferences. These bigger events, though often pricey, expose you to the latest and greatest ideas in EdTech and also allow you to meet new people and build that PLN. And yet, they can be a bit intimidating if you're new to the conference scene.

If you're like me, you arrive excited, caffeinated, and ready to learn new tricks and tips and leave with sore feet, a full brain, and an overwhelming laundry list of things to try. Hopefully, your departure is fueled with inspiration, but most conference-goers I chat with cite *overwhelmed* as their primary emotion.

So how to avoid this feeling? How do you go to an event chock-full of other excited educators brimming with ideas and leave with a manageable task list? Here are some tips I use to help me leave these conferences feeling fulfilled yet focused:

Step 1. Go With a Goal in Mind

I try to attend events with a current nagging problem of practice or goal in mind. That way, when I look at the amazing schedule of sessions, I can be a bit smarter about where to go. And moreover, I listen with a specific challenge in mind. I find this helps me stay focused and allows me to leave feeling more accomplished.

Step 2. Keep a Three-Dance Card

Too often, I go to sessions and leave with an ever-growing list of things to try but no time to try them. (Side note: Try a PLAYDATE if you're looking for more playtime.) So now I go with a three-dance card—that is, a note with three slots. As I hear about new and exciting things, I write them on my dance card to try when I get home. When I get to a fourth "cool new thing" I need to decide to bump an already penciled-in tool or strategy or forgo it. Although this was difficult at first, it was so liberating to leave with three big ideas to try out when I got home instead of dozens. And you know what? Whereas I never tried out the dozens upon returning home, I've consistently dug into my three-dance card list because it is so much more manageable.

Step 3. Recruit Allies and Use Collaborative Tools

Do you ever feel the Sophie's choice of deciding where to go when looking at a particularly rich session schedule? I do. If you came with a team, select multiple sessions that interest you and split up—but not before setting up collaborative Google Docs. If each of you attends a session and takes extensive notes on shared Docs—complete with photos and links—you can virtually attend each other's sessions. Even more, you can jump into one another's Docs during a slow part of your session and feed them questions to ask their presenters at the end. If you went with Tip #1 and created individual goals or problems of practice preconference, the note taker can keep this in mind when jotting down pertinent facts from their session. So boom—multiple sessions attended at once = #timetravel.

If you didn't come with a team, consider making some new friends. Or even if you did come with a team, still consider making new friends. Take a moment at the conference to look up from your screens and say hello to the person next to you. Most conference goers breeze through their sessions doing their best not to talk to anyone else—sitting far from others, finding lone spaces at lunch, texting in the corner between sessions. In these cases, we're missing out on the best potential learning at these conferences—each other. The people who decided to wake up early and attend this event most likely have similar challenges, goals, and passions. Striking up a chat between sessions may just lead to an incredible connection. Who knows? That person might be your edusoulmate! I speak from experience. A few years ago, I connected with five other educators at a conference and we realized we had a lot in common—so we combined our powers and passions to create the types of professional development we wanted for ourselves. These are the very folks with whom I went on to cofound PLAYDATE!

Step 4. Schedule Time With Yourself to Debrief Individually

It's important that you take time not only to attend these professional learning events but also to debrief with yourself afterward. Schedule a coffee or tea date for yourself about a week after the event to review your notes, try out tools, or make next steps. Too often, we return from these professional learning sojourns only to get sucked into the quick-paced cadence of the real world and lose sight of much of the learning and inspiration we gained while away.

Step 5. Pay It Forward

And perhaps most importantly, don't forget to #payitforward. It's a treat to take a few days away to learn and grow professionally, and not all our colleagues get to enjoy this. So schedule time to share, be it formally during a school professional development meeting or unofficially over drinks with friends. Hey, I've even started meeting for breakfast with colleagues (#edtechNeggs) because breakfast is the only meal we can all manage. No matter how you do it, be sure to share.

··· Seven-Day Challenge ···

Already rocked that TIEP? Wanting to try something else but not ready to dig into another problem of practice? Try this seven-day challenge to power up and prepare for your next innovation exploration plan! Seven days mean seven challenges, an hour for each challenge.

(1) **Go on a blog bender:** Blogs are important sources of professional learning for teachers—read blogs, subscribe to them, go to them when you're stuck or in need of inspiration. For those of you who are already reading blogs, this challenge is partly about finding new ones; for those who have yet to enjoy a good education blog, start fresh. See the companion website for a list of my current favorites.

However, reading blogs is only half of this challenge. The other half is to create your own blog, if you don't yet have one. This is a perfect way for both experts and newbies

(Continued)

(Continued)

alike to share their journey with others and themselves. A blog can be a reflective tool, allowing you to look back on your day, week, or even month and think about what worked and what didn't, what you learned and what questions still remain. For some ideas for blog hosting sites, check out http://wordpress.com, http://kidblog.org, and http://blogger.com.

(2) **Commit to a conference:** Conferences are fun ways to connect with other passionate educators in person. Like summer camp for adults, these events offer inspirational messages, hands-on workshops, and playtime in the form of socials and happy hours. This challenge is about exploring the different conferences that are coming up and signing up for one—or three! Here are three you can take a look at to get started:

- http://isteconference.org
- http://gafesummit.com
- http://edcamp.wikispaces.com

After you've done this, blog about it! Share what conference you'll be attending, why you chose it, and what you want to learn.

(3) **Virtual learning marathon:** To bone up on educational technology ideas before your conference, go on a virtual learning marathon. This challenge asks you to dig into YouTube playlists to find short tutorials, Google's Education Courses, and iTunes University to explore new concepts or get geeky on some you already know. Want to do this one while cleaning the house, going for a run on the lake, or driving your kids to camp? Check out the following podcasts on EdReach (available for download to your mobile phone)!

- http://bit.ly/chad20sec
- http://bit.ly/jaddons
- http://edreach.us
- http://google.com/edu
- http://bit.ly/itunesulink

And then . . . blog! Write about what you learned from this marathon and what you want to learn next. Share the best videos you found and why they were useful. Help others to get what you just got!

(4) **Curate digital content:** Not all digital content is about professional learning. A lot of videos out there are aimed directly at students. Take some time to preview some content and save the gems you find for the fall. Use the amazing EduClipper site (similar to Pinterest but made just for educators) to keep track of what you find

and to see what others are finding useful. Some examples of sites you can examine also include http://youtube.com/education and http://blog.mrmeyer.com.

Guess what you should do now . . . blog! Share your EduClipper; explain what you loved and what didn't work for you. Even describe some rough ideas for how you might use these tools in the fall.

(5) **Take on a Twitter chat:** Speaking of others, get connected this summer. Meet new folks who are interested in similar topics and face similar challenges—all without changing out of your pajamas! Twitter chats allow folks from all over the world to discuss issues that matter to them. By using Twitter hashtags, chat moderators can host a roundtable session based around specific topics like #1stchat (first grade teachers), #mathchat (math teachers), and so on. They happen on a certain day each week, at a certain time, and are usually an hour in length. For a list of Twitter chats and the times they meet, check out the ever-updating list that Jerry Blumengarten (@cybraryman1) created at http://www.cybraryman.com/edhashtags.html. And yes . . . you should definitely blog about this.

(6) **Three little goals:** Day 6 already! You've already completed five challenges at this point. You've gathered ideas and digital content, committed to continued learning at a conference, and started your own blog. Now it's time to figure out how you're going to apply this learning in the fall. Create three goals for new things you'd like to try this school year. Start small—smaller goals are those that you're more likely to do. Make sure you know how you will achieve this goal and have a timeline. Set deadlines for your goals; create calendar appointments in whatever calendars you use to remind yourself of when to get started. Then . . . share it on a blog so the world can help you with tips and encouragement!

(7) **First day war plan:** Now that you've got some goals and learning in the chute, it's time to revisit your TIEP. What's the next problem of practice you want to tackle? Challenge yourself to try something loftier this time and shoot for the moon. And of course . . . share your plan on your blog!

chapter 15

PLANNING YOUR NEXT EDVENTURE

It's time to say goodbye, but I think goodbyes are sad and I'd much rather say hello. Hello to a new adventure.

—Ernie Harwell

Whether you decided to read this entire book cover-to-cover or skipped around and landed here, I have one final message for you: Don't stop edventuring.

In my first journey, I was thrilled to see my students' creativity reborn, their eyes lighting up for the first time in years. The explorations we shared and learning opportunities we discovered were incredible. These wins were a source of euphoria for me as an educator, and it would have been simple for me to say, "Innovation—check. Done. Nailed it."

But I also knew that there is always more to do, more to learn, more to try. Our classrooms must grow and evolve to meet the fluctuating needs of our students and take advantage of the ever-changing array of technological tools. Let's go back to our original metaphor of the ancient Polynesian sailors. We acknowledge that yes, the feat they accomplished of utilizing both the science and art of navigation to traverse the vast seas is amazing. We also acknowledge that it was incredible how they convinced others to take this journey with them who originally resisted the adventure. And yet, there's still something else: Once they reached those impossible destinations of remote islands far into the Pacific, they didn't stop there. They continued on to a new and even more impossible challenge.

So as you take what you learned from this book and implement it in your classroom, as you FAIL[1] and then SAIL[2] with your students, here are a few final tips to keep you moving forward to the next edventure.

---

[1] First Attempt In Learning; see Chapter 5 on embracing failure.

[2] Subsequent Attempt In Learning; see Chapter 5 on embracing failure.

BE YOUR OWN HERO

Don't forget to celebrate yourself and your small wins. This journey can be long and arduous. Even if you go into it with an "I accept failure" attitude, it can still be disheartening not to see immediate full-scale success. So look for the areas that *are* working. Find things for which you can congratulate yourself and your students. If you're blogging, share it out loud for the world to hear. Too often, I hear colleagues say, "I'm just a teacher." No, you're not. You're the front line for shaping our future. Remember that every day you wake up and work with students is a day of success, even if you're still working toward bigger goals.

DON'T GET COMFORTABLE

After the days, weeks, and even months of struggle it will take you and your students to reach a place of "I got this," it will be easy to want to stop to catch your breath. That's fine—take a moment to savor the hard-earned success of realizing your own version of innovation. However, don't let this be the end. The moment you begin to think "Wow, this is actually pretty easy" that should be your trigger to start seeking a new problem of practice to tackle. The scientist Astro Teller once said, "Our ambitions are a glass ceiling in what we can accomplish." I love this quote and agree completely. And yet, I believe that we have layers of glass ceilings. Each time we set our ambitions higher, there's yet another pane of glass to crash through.

CHANNEL YOUR INNER STUDENT

For many teachers, being an educator is so much more than a job. It's who we are as people. My husband is an attorney. Very rarely does he introduce himself by saying, "Hi, my name is Jim; I'm a lawyer." However, I almost always let people know in our first interactions that I'm a proud educator. It's who I am and it makes me happy. As I write this, I'm coming home from working with a group of students who were sharing their ideas of a new and improved school system. One piece of advice I heard over and over again from this group is one that I preach myself: Teachers need to have fun.

Think about the last time you enjoyed a concert, show, or even a professional learning event. Usually, the people leading the event seemed like they were having a great time. Perhaps the band was jamming and joking with each other and the audience. Perhaps the comedian was cracking up at his own jokes. Maybe the presenter seemed completely passionate and excited by her topic. If we want our students to enjoy being in school, we need to model this joy ourselves.

Find the glee in your day and don't be afraid to let it show in front of your students. As one of the astute young men said to me, "Teachers need to relax and have more fun with us. We know they're human. They just need to show it more often."

SHARE YOUR CRAZY PILLS

Now that you've unlocked the secrets of innovation by reading this book (wink, wink), pay it forward. Share this with the restless natives on your island. Now it's your turn to convince them to jump in your boat and join the edventure. How can you spread this mindset in your school or setting? What problem of practice did you find in Part II that would help a particular colleague? You don't have to ask them to run out and buy this book, but consider giving them some ideas from it, loaning it to them, or simply sharing some suggestions with them face-to-face over a cup of coffee.

After all, it's a great feeling to successfully embark on your own edventure. What's even more exciting is when others decide to join you on subsequent journeys. You'll find that as everyone begins to discover his or her own Innovation Island, they begin to form together into a bigger Innovation Land Mass. Soon, you'll wake up to find that you're no longer alone in the sea of crazy but surrounded by your tribe: fellow edventurers who are as passionate about increasing student opportunity as you.

People always ask me, "What do you predict the classroom of the future will look like?" I always reply, if I could predict the future classroom, I'd be sorely disappointed. I love being surprised by new developments in technology and pedagogy. I love seeing the impossible become commonplace. The search for classroom innovation is an ongoing expedition, and I can't wait to see what tomorrow's discovery brings.

#COURAGEOUSEDVENTURES

Appendix A: Blank Challenge Cards

CHALLENGE:

Card A: Front

If you think the answer is:

_____ - go to card B

_____ - go to card C

_____ - go to card D

Card A: Back

Card B

Card B: Front

Finished early?

Try _____

_____

_____

_____

Card B: Back

Card C

Card C: Front

Finished early?

Try _____

_____

_____

_____

Card C: Back

Card D

Card D: Front

Finished early?

Try _____

_____

_____

_____

Card D: Back

APPENDIX B

Teacher Innovation Exploration Plan (TIEP)

PROBLEM OF PRACTICE

Problem Description (be as detailed as possible)

Past Solutions

What you've already tried	What worked	What didn't work

NEW SOLUTION

New Solution	
What you need to accomplish this	**Support you need (and from whom)**

Action Plan

Action Item	Step-by-Step to Do List	Due Date	Needs / Notes / Reflection

FINAL REFLECTION

What worked	What didn't work
What will you do differently next time?	

INDEX

Adaptive learning programs, 20–21 (box)

Assessment strategies
    badging systems, 81–84, 82 (figure)
    digital response software, 67–68
    feedback, 78–80, 79 (figures), 88
    gamification, 81
    IEPs and, 69–70
    learning management systems and, 68–69
    metacognitive screencasting, 70,
        71–72 (box)
    online forms, 69
    student self-assessment, 70–78

Audri's Monster Trap, 111

Badging systems, 81–84, 82 (figure)

Behavioral issues
    promotion of positive actions, 88
    support for struggling students, 91–92
    See also Digital citizenship

Bellow, Adam, 96

Blogging, 80, 91, 95, 98, 123–124, 147–149,
    148 (figure)

Blumengarten, Jerry, 98

Brookhouser, Kevin, 116

Bucciantini, Carl, 141

Challenge Card activity, 61–62, 62 (figure)

Chanel, Coco, 143

Children's Online Privacy Protection Act
    (COPPA), 32, 33–34 (figure), 35

Class Dojo tool, 88, 88 (figure),
    89 (figure), 93

Classroom environments
    communication goals, 121–122
    digital newsletters/blogs, 95
    mood check-ins, 87, 87 (figure),
        88 (figure)
    music and, 89–91
    positive behavior encouragement, 88
    respect and, 86 (box)
    struggling students and, 91–92

Class websites, 66, 95

Common Sense Media, 37

Communication
    classroom discussions, 126–129,
        127 (figure), 128 (figure)
    classroom goals in, 121–122
    between home and school, 93–94,
        93 (figure), 94 (figures)
    innervoice, 123–124, 124–126 (box)
    social media, 129–132, 130–131 (box)
    See also Blogging

Copyright concerns, 37, 38 (figure)

Couros, George, 4

Creative Commons, 38 (figure)

Creativity, importance of, 47, 104–105
    See also Purposeful playtime

Critical Friend
    for students, 64
    for teachers, 25–26, 144

Cummings, E. E., 103

Curiosity cultivation, 106, 107–110,
    108 (figure)

Curriculum development
    curricular resources, 96–98
    vertical alignment strategies, 99–100,
        100 (figure), 101 (figure)

Cyberbullying, 37

Device management system, 40–42

Differentiated learning
    assessment strategies, 69–70
    content creation, 64–65
    digital workflow, 65–66
    online resources, 65
    rotation model, 51–52 (box)
    student engagement strategies, 60–64
    video lessons and, 57–58

Digital citizenship
    cyberbullying, 37
    data privacy, 32, 33–34 (figure), 35–36
    importance of, 32
    student misconduct issues, 37, 44–45,
        45–46 (box)

Digital divide, 6, 6 (figure)

Digital footprint, 35–36

Digital newsletters, 95

Digital portfolios

creation considerations, 74
digital tools for, 72–74
Google Drawings, use of, 75–78,
    75 (figure), 76 (figures), 77 (figure)
Digital technology
  accessories and supplies, 42–43
  cost considerations, 46
  device and software choices,
    xvi–xvii (box)
  device management, 40–42
  for digital portfolio creation, 72–74
  digital response software, 67–68
  integration tools, 8–12, 8 (figure),
    10 (figure)
  teacher learning experiences,
    156–157 (box)
  video content, 57–60
Doodle.com, 98
"Do Schools Kill Creativity?" TED Talk
  (Robinson), 47, 104

EdCamp model, 154
Edmodo, 66
Educational hashtags, 97–98
EduClipper, 96–97
Engagement strategies, 60–64
Explain Everything app, 30–31 (box)

FAIL (First Attempt In Learning) acronym,
  48, 111
Failure
  digital system, 52–53, 52 (figure)
  failing forward, 48
  FAIL-to-SAIL blogs, 111–112
  fear and, 47–48
  perseverance and, 110–111
  student, 49–50
  teacher, 50–51, 51–52 (box)
Family Educational Rights and Privacy Act
  (FERPA), 32, 33–34 (figure)
Feedback, 25–26, 78–80, 79 (figures)
Flipped classroom model, 51–52 (box)

Gamification, 81
The Gift of Failure (Lahey), 112
Google, 59 (box)
Google Calendar, 98, 100 (figure),
  101 (figure)
Google Classroom, 66
Google Drawings, 75–78, 75 (figure),
  76 (figures), 77 (figure), 91–92
Google Drive, 78, 79 (figure), 80, 99–100
Google Forms, 80, 93–94, 94 (figures)
Google Hangouts, 99

Gorman, Sue, 154
Gripe Jam activity, 14, 17, 19–20

Harwell, Ernie, 162
Heath, Chip, 105
Heath, Dan, 105

Individualized Education Programs (IEPs),
  69–70
Innovation, 4–7
  See also Innovation, problem-based;
    Innovation, student
Innovation, problem-based
  action plan tips, 22–23,
    23–25 (figure)
  problem identification, 20–21 (box)
  purpose of, 13–14
  reflection, 119–120
  solution focus in, 21–22
  Teacher Innovation Exploration Plan
    (TIEP), 14–21, 15 (figure),
    16 (figure), 18 (figures),
    19 (figures), 23–24 (figure), 96
  tips, 162–164
Innovation, student
  creativity and, 104–105
  curiosity and, 107–110
  perseverance and, 111–112
  purposeful play and, 115–119
  student teams, 27–30, 30–31 (box)
The Innovator's Mindset (Couros), 4
International Society for Technology in
  Education (ISTE), 152

Kahoot website, 68
Kidblog, 80
KidTREK app, 139–140 (box)

Lahey, Jessica, 112
Laidler, Autumn, 154
Learning management systems, 65–66,
  68–69
Leonard, Jamila, 130–131 (box)
Lesson planning, video, 57–58
Lynch, Jenny, 130–131 (box)

Mandela, Nelson, 55
Metacognitive screencasting, 70,
  71–72 (box)
Motivation, types of, 83
Mouse Squad, 30
Music usage in classroom, 89–91

National Teachers Academy, 6

OK Go band, 112–115 (box)
Open scheduling, 116–117

Perseverance, 106
Personalized learning, 67
Pinterest, 96
Play. *See* Purposeful playtime
PLAYDATE model, 154–155
Plickers app, 68
Privacy concerns, 32, 33–34 (figure),
  35–36
Problem-based innovation. *See* Innovation,
  problem-based
Problem-based learning
  challenge development, 136
  completion of challenges, 138, 140
  description of, 13, 133–134, 133 (figure)
  problem/challenge identification, 135
  reflection, 137, 138 (figure)
  teachers' role in, 138–139
Professional learning network
  development of, 151–152
  EdTech learning, 156–157 (box)
  professional conference attendance,
    157–159
  teacher-led learning events, 153–156
Project-based learning, 133 (figure), 134
Public presentation tips, 149–150
Puentedura, Ruben, 8
Purposeful playtime, 106
  creative options, 117–119
  open scheduling, 116–117
  reimagined centers, 116
  20% time, 105, 116

Quadblogging, 80
Questions, types of, 107–110,
  108 (figure), 135
Quizlet app, 68

Recognition badges, 81
Richards, Reshan, 31
Robinson, Ken, 47, 104–105
Rome, Amy, 6
Rube Goldberg machines, 111

SAIL (Subsequent Attempts In Learning)
  acronym, 48, 111
SAMR Model, 8–9, 8 (figure), 11, 144–145
Schoology, 66
Shedd, John A., 1
Shelton, Ken, 48
Social media, 97–98, 129–132,
  130–131 (box)

Socrative website, 68
Student engagement, 60–64
  See also Innovation, student
Student leadership teams
  device management tasks, 39–40
  peer-to-peer tech help, 27–30,
    30–31 (box)
Stylus, 42, 43 (figure)
Switch (Heath & Heath), 105

Teacher collaboration and support,
  25–26, 98–99
  See also Professional learning network
Teacher conferences, 140–141
Teacher Innovation Exploration Plan,
  14–21, 15 (figure), 16 (figure),
  18 (figures), 19 (figures),
  23–24 (figure)
  See also Innovation, problem-based
Team planning, 98–99
Technology Integration Matrix (TIM),
  9–12, 9n5, 10 (figure),
  144–146
Technology integration tools, 8–12,
  8 (figure), 10 (figure)
TECHVibe student blog, 124–126 (box)
Teller, Astro, 163
Time management
  open scheduling, 116–117
  purposeful playtime, 115–119
  team planning, 98–99
  20% time strategy, 105, 116
The 20Time Project (Brookhouser),
  116, 139
20% time strategy, 105, 116
Twitter, 97, 129, 130–131 (box), 142

U.S. Department of Education's National
  Education Technology Plan, 6

Video content
  annotation tools, 63, 63 (figure)
  creation tips, 59–60
  for lesson planning, 57–58
  metacognitive screencasting,
    70, 71–72 (box)
  organization and storage,
    58–59 (box)
Vimeo, 59 (box)
Virtual meetings, 99

YouTube, 59 (box), 63, 63 (figure)

Ziemke, Kristin, 141

CORWIN
A SAGE Publishing Company

Helping educators make the greatest impact

CORWIN HAS ONE MISSION: to enhance education through intentional professional learning.

We build long-term relationships with our authors, educators, clients, and associations who partner with us to develop and continuously improve the best evidence-based practices that establish and support lifelong learning.

Solutions you want. Experts you trust. Results you need.